# The
# JUDGEMENTS
# OF GOD

## DR. GILBERT H. EDWARDS, SR.

authorHOUSE®

*AuthorHouse*™
*1663 Liberty Drive*
*Bloomington, IN 47403*
*www.authorhouse.com*
*Phone: 1 (800) 839-8640*

*Published by AuthorHouse   01/13/2015*

*ISBN: 978-1-4969-6335-2 (sc)*
*ISBN: 978-1-4969-6336-9 (hc)*
*ISBN: 978-1-4969-6334-5 (e)*

*Library of Congress Control Number: 2015900283*

*Any people depicted in stock imagery provided by Thinkstock are models, and such images are being used for illustrative purposes only. Certain stock imagery © Thinkstock.*

*This book is printed on acid-free paper.*

*Scripture quotations marked KJV are from the Holy Bible, King James Version (Authorized Version). First published in 1611. Quoted from the KJV Classic Reference Bible, Copyright © 1983 by The Zondervan Corporation.*

Dedicated

To

All My Readers

And

All Law Breakers of

The

Word of God

# PREFACE

I feel that there is a need for me to write concerning the Judgments of God. There are many judgments that are being displayed daily. People sometimes judge one another, also God, the Judge of all Judges, now on a small scale, but still there will be a final judgment called "The Great White Throne Judgment."

The scriptures anticipate a coming judgment by God on all men. Such was the expectation of the Psalmist as he wrote in Psalm 96:13; "Before the Lord: For He cometh, for He cometh to judge the earth: he shall judge the world with righteousness, and the people with His truth." "Because He hath appointed a day in the which he will judge the world in righteousness by that man whom He hath ordained; whereof He hath given assurance unto all men, in that He hath raised Him from the dead." (Acts 17:31)

# CONTENTS

# INTRODUCTION

The subject of "Judgment" is a large one in the word of God and encompasses such, as the judgment of the cross, the judgment on the believer in chastening, the self judgment of the believer, the judgment of the believer's works, at the judgment seat of Christ, with the exception of the last mentioned judgment, which has already been considered. These judgments are not related with the eschatological program of God. It is necessary to consider four judgments that have eschatological implications: the judgment on the nation Israel, the judgment of the nations, the judgment of the fallen angels and the judgment of the Great White Throne.

This study will give explanatory reasons for these judgments. God will bring every deed into judgment including every hidden thing, whether it is good or evil. God's judgment is thorough. He considers every deed even the secret things. His judgment is fair. He considers both the good things done and the evil. In the judgments of God, the wicked and the good are showed in scriptures, that the evil are punished and the good are rewarded. The judgment of God upon the wicked is certain. No nation, no matter how proud and powerful, can stand. God's people will yet be vindicated in their struggle with evil forces.

God allows the evil forces of satan to exercise control and inflict judgment, but their time of power has been limited by Him long before they gain power. God controls time and eternity. Satan does not. God's saints must endure such difficult times with patience and faith.

The Order of Events from the Rapture of the Church
Through the Great White Throne Judgment

After the rapture, which is when the Church will be taken out of the world, (I Thessalonians 3:17) will begin the tribulation period. The Tribulation is seven years which is the seventy weeks of Daniel (Daniel 9:24-27). Within the seven years of the Tribulation period there are many events, first the invasion of God and Magog in the beginning of the Tribulation (Ezekiel 38 & 39). I believe that Ezekiel makes it clear that the invasion in Chapter 38 is not the same as the battle of Gog and Magog at the end of the Millennial. Secondly, near the end of the Tribulation will be the event of the Battle of Armageddon (Revelation 19:19). The armies at Armageddon are destroyed by the sword that goes out of Christ's mouth (Revelation 19:15). Thirdly, the Tribulation ends with the second coming of Christ. Between the Battle of Gog and Magog and the Battle of Armageddon, the two Babylonians are destroyed, and the antichrist and false prophet are cast into the Lake of Fire.

Following the Tribulation is the Millennial. Satan is bounded for 1,000 years (Revelation 20:1-2). The Millennium will be the period of the full manifestation of the Glory of the Lord Jesus Christ. There will be the Glory of a glorious dominion, in which Christ, by virtue of His obedience unto death, is given universal dominion ot replace that dominion which Adam lost. There will be the Glory of a glorious government in which Christ, as David's son, is given absolute power to govern (Isaiah 9:6; 11:4). Also, there will be the Glory of a glorious inheritance, in which the land and the seed promised to Abraham are realized through Christ (Genesis 17:8; Daniel 11:16). When the 1,000 years are expired, Satan shall be loosed out of his prison, (Revelation 20:7) and deceive the nations which are in the four quarters of the earth, Gog and Magog to gather them together to battle (Revelation 20:8), but fire came down from God out of heaven and devoured them (vs. 9).

Finally, the Great White Throne Judgment, which is the judgment on sinners at the Great White Throne, also the earth is purged by fire (Revelations 10-11). In verse 12, the unbelieving dead are judged out of the Books of Works and the Book of Life.

# CHAPTER I
# THE HISTORY OF JUDGMENT

The Judgment of God comes certainly, if not swiftly, when we disobey God. Sometimes God moves swiftly in bringing judgment. Sometimes He moves slowly; but He always moves to judge sin. God prefers that His judgment be positive and redemptive rather than negative and vindictive. Even in judgment, God is loving rather than vengeful. God tempered His judgment of Adam and Eve by providing more adequate clothing for them than they could provide for themselves. Though He drove them out of their sheltered place in the Garden, they were not driven beyond the reach of His loving concern for their well-being. Their work now became difficult toil, and life was to be punctuated by suffering. Life was still possible in God's world. God would still give them a harvest for their labor. The whole story of redemption that emerges as the bible progresses is proof of God's continuing interest in people despite their sin. God's judgment should be understood in the light of His grace. If His judgments were not tempered by His grace, there would be no salvation of any of us. When God created man, moral laws operated in God's creation. Rebellion against God brings punishment and ultimate death. Human dominion over creation is not absolute. God sets limits which humans must obey or suffer the consequences. Creation is God's gift and retains an element of God's mystery which humans can never know. The doctrine of creation presents a call to humans to trust God and not seek absolute freedom. Human pain, broken relationships, a non-productive environment and occupational toil are all related to human rebellion and not to God's original intention for human life. They represent God's gracious alternative to the expected sentence of immediate death. The Creator set up a moral world in which wrong doing ultimately receives its proper recompense. He also reacted and reacts to wrong doing in grace, providing hope even in light of human sin. God loved His creation; but when it defied His moral standards, He knew the He must vindicate His holiness by sending punishment. Because creation was good; however, He wished to preserve it. He established propagation as He method of perpetuating His creation. Even as He punishes sinners, He made provision for propagation of the species to continue. We can be certain that God's world will go on today until He wills to consummate history with Christ's return. The world is so constituted that it adjusts to any shock or tragedy. God controls creation's destiny.

Judgment is part of God's history; for humans do not consistently cooperate to achieve God's purposes. God works in history to eliminate that which ignores His moral will. Judgment occurs in communication with God's faithful people, and in mercy. In historical judgment, God's people see the holy, righteous and just side of God's character. The righteousness of God prompted Him to consider bringing judgment upon the extreme wickedness of Sodom and Gomorrah. On the other hand, Abraham's plea for righteous people who might live in the City evoked the promise of God that if just ten righteous were found there, God would spare the cities. This does not mean that the wicked would go unpunished. It does not mean that God would not destroy the righteous in a destruction meant as judgment for the wicked. Sparing ten righteous persons had a greater value in God's eyes than destroying all of the wicked of the two cities. Judgment is held in reserve until people reject grace and redemption. A righteous God must act justly. God Himself is the standard of justice. It is the very nature of God to do what is right in all circumstances. God will do what is right in all circumstances. God will not do what is wrong, for that which would contradict His own nature and will. We cannot always easily determine what is right and what is wrong in any given set of circumstances. We can rest assured that God, in His infinite wisdom, will always do what is right. God's wrath comes in judgment upon those who do not repent of their sins and turn to Him. How soon that judgment comes and how that wrath is expressed is not for us to determine. God's judgment came dramatically and decisively on Sodom and Gomorrah.

The fact that God has not dealt just as openly and dramatically with other persons or cities does not mean that God will not act in judgment on them. In His grace, God often delays the exercise of His wrath to let His grace achieve positive results. God attempts through His grace and His wrath to bring people to repentance, faith, and responsible action. The wrath of God is the last resort. It is neither right nor loving for God to simply let sin go unpunished in the lives of those who will not respond to Him in faith. It is not right because God does not contradict His own basic character by continuing to overlook sin. It is not love because God will not let people have reason to believe sin is not serious. God's actions lead us to take Him seriously when He demands our repentance and right living. God's intervention can present sin against His people even though they deceive and are guilty.

Living in a sinful environment does not justify deception. Nor does it justify expecting God to save us from the consequences of our sin. God may act to achieve His purpose, but is not bound to act just because we claim to be His people. God's justice is not a blind, arbitrary, mechanical reaction to evil or the appearance of evil. God's justice take into account the circumstances involved in each individual situation. Instead of pouring harsh judgment upon Abimelech for unwittingly taking Abraham's wife, God tempered His judgment with understanding and mercy. We can always count on God to understand our circumstances at any given time. He is a loving heavenly Father, just as Jesus taught. This does not mean that we can manipulate God or make flimsy excuses for our disobedience. God's justice is informed by His perfect knowledge of us. We cannot deceive God, but we can depend upon Him to deal with us justly.

Even the elements of nature moved to bring judgment and punishment upon Pharoah and those who disobeyed God, so He could reveal His election power and purpose to foreign people in a foreign land. Sin and unbelief lead to the doctrine of election, where in God selects, delivers and trains people to be His own in the midst of an unbelieving world. Although God is gracious, loving and patient, He also judges rebellious, sinful people. Those who refuse His salvation and stubbornly reject His will inevitably experience God's judgment. Their lives result in ruin:

> "The Lord wailing throughout Egypt over the death of Egypt's first born sons contrasted with the silence and peace of both persons and animals, even the dogs in Israel. This indicated that God is a God of distinction and choice. His people are the chosen or elected ones free from the wrath experienced by those who saw Pharaoh as Lord. Even Pharaoh was helpless in saving his firstborn son, the heir apparent to Pharaoh's throne of power." (Exodus 11:7)

God does not view sin lightly. If God's people do not take Him seriously, if they do not honor Him as Lord, if they do not follow His commandment, then they can expect to suffer His wrath poured out in judgment upon them. God pours out His wrath not simply to punish, but to bring people to responsible obedience. We are not free under God to pick and choose among His commands. God, not we, decides what is right and what is wrong, what is good for us and what is bad. Any violation of God's covenant is considered to be an act of rebellion against Him, and therefore, a sin. Obedience produces a full and meaningful life; disobedience produces an empty and meaningless existence. Breaking God's commands brings deserved divine judgment. Judgment on sin is a part of God's covenant. Although judgment in the form of exile from the land would occur, God promises to continue in covenant relationship with His people and return them to the land (Leviticus 26:40-45). God at times chooses to use history as the arena to display His power and justice in judging His disobedient people. Judgment for sin can come even to a people God forgives (Numbers 14:17-38). History calls for special obedience to God's directions in light of past discipline and past suffering.

God's historical acts do not automatically bring revelation or salvation. God must enable a person to recognize historical events as His actors and to accept Him as Lord because of those acts. God acts so people may know Him. Constant repetition of and meditation on such acts should lead to faith with such understanding does not take credit for understanding, knowing that even the ability to understand came from God. Persons who do not learn from God's acts and respond in obedience to His will know they deserve the judgment that comes upon them. God prepares us to expect His punishment for sin and provides His teaching to lead us back to Him. God told Moses to write a song so His people would eventually realize that their suffering was His punishment for their sins. Often, God's judgment is preparation to show compassion and love to the remnant of His people. (Deuteronomy 31:14-32:49) God acted in history to give Israel the land He had promised. In acting, He expected Israel to do their part in faith and obedience. When they disobeyed, anger and judgment followed. In His historical acts, God remained free to punish a disobedient people. His promises and their expectations of victory did not prevent God from disciplining disobedient people. Such judgment called forth praise and confession, not retreat and abandonment of the mission (Joshua 7:1-26). Refusal to obey God despite His historical evidence of power and faithfulness brought suspension of God's promise to defeat their enemies. The relationship with God is an on-going historical commitment, not a one-time ceremonial ritual. It is a responsibility for every generation; not a birthright of a race. Forgetting God's acts for His people can lead a generation to forget and ignore God. That brings His anger and judgment. (Judges 2:1-15)

God's presence symbolized by the Ark brought judgment on the unbelieving Philistines and on irreverent Israelites. News, of the details of the Exodus, was known by the Philistines and motivated their action. They knew some events were directly caused by God, while others were chance happenings according to the natural rules of human and international relationships. God showed that He had caused judgment on the Philistines (I Samuel 6:1-20). Political leaders are not and must not presume to be God. All human power structures stand under God's control and judgment. God expects leaders to seek and obey His will, when they do not, they face His punishment. Saul's disobedience of God's command led to the loss of his kingdom (I Samuel 15:10-29). Historical human actions affect the relationship with God. Divine anger eventually finds expression in historical acts of judgment. History is the story of relationships between God and the people He created. Any way of explaining historical events that ignore God is a method dealing with secondary causes rather than primary causes. God called history into being and will ultimately bring it to an end. He never leaves history to its own interests and agents. He maintains interest in every moment of human history.

> "From there, Elisha went up to Bethel. As he was walking along the road, some youths came out of the town and jeered at him. 'Go on up, you baldhead!', they said. 'Go on up, you baldhead!' He turned around, looked at them and called down a curse on them in the name of the Lord. Then two bears came out of the woods and mauled forty-two of the youths. And he went on to Mount Carmel and from there returned to Samaria. (II Kings 2:23-25)"

This brief description of judgment on the disrespectful young lads appears unduly harsh. The bear came out of the woods after Elisha had cursed the lads "in the name of the Lord." Elisha showed the strong hand of God in judgment. The prophetic word controlled Israel's history. The rise and fall of international powers occurred as God announced them through His prophets. God promised judgment on a people who followed other gods, and after two centuries of enduring their false worship in mercy, He fulfilled His threats (II Kings 17:3-23). The history of the Northern Kingdom teaches one major lesson: God will intervene in human history to punish His unfaithful people because He takes sin seriously. Israel followed neighbors and kings – everyone but God. They knew they were doing wrong. They tried to hide from God. They openly violated their covenant agreement with Him. They refused to listen to His chosen ministers sent to warn them. Everything they did showed they trusted their judgment instead of God's word. They became a worthless people in God's eyes, incapable of carrying out His purposes. The Israelites faced exile because of their determination to step over God's explicit moral boundaries. Their choices for worship and life-style values demonstrated poor judgment. Your life-style is shaped by whom and what you worship. Life is too important to waste it on idolatrous ways.

The most faithful of God's people make mistakes. King David's command was evil and brought God's judgment (I Chronicles 21:7). In judging His people, God remained responsive to them. He retracted the announcement of total abandonment when leaders of His people humbly returned to Him. He used judgment to show His people the privilege they have in serving Him.

The wrath of God was announced against Judah for the worship of false gods as reported in Chapter 11 of the Book of II Chronicles. Because they humbled themselves, this judgment was tempered with mercy. This shows us wrath is not an absolute decree made by God, but is a personal response to the actions of His people (II Chronicles 12:5-12). A people unfaithful to God face turbulence and distress. God works through international crises to teach His people their need for faithfulness. Jealousy among family members and the desire for power incited violent attacks upon other members of the family and among the rulers in Israel and Judah. Jehoram, son of Jehoshaphat, slaughtered his brothers along with other princes of Israel to avert any threat to the throne. His sin brought God's judgment upon his family and upon himself. (II Chronicles 21:12-20) Judgment for sin can come immediately upon God's people when they disregard Him and His word. To forsake God is to abandon Him in favor of other priorities. Forsaking God leads to forsaking all moral principles. To forsake God is to execute judgment upon you. God warns His people of the consequences of sin before He exercises judgment. Such warning is available in His word, in the lesson of history, and through the message of His chosen ministers. God follows His warning with action. (II Chronicles 24:20)

God's people find material success difficult to handle. Uzziah let pride blind him to the true source of his success. He refused to accept the limits of his office and suffered God's judgment. (II Chronicles 26:16-21) God's judgment is discipline seeking to turn His people back to Him. When people respond to judgment in repentance, God responds in grace. Both deliverance and judgment in history seek to lead people to confess God, as they only God, and to serve Him faithfully. In grace, God calls His people to repent and be faithful. Eventually, He exercises His wrath to bring historical judgment. Ignoring or mocking God's word invites God's wrath. Deliverance and judgment throughout history teaches God's people His justice and faithfulness. History becomes the content of a prayer of confession and a prayer for new deliverance. Note the close relationship between the idea of the righteousness of God and God acting as judge of all the earth. His judgment will be carried out on the basis of righteousness. His righteous judgment brings joy and praise to His creation. (Psalms 96:10-13)

The future for mankind, both the good and the bad sinner, is in God's hands. Left to discover it for themselves, persons might conclude death ends it all for everyone. The text, as in much of Ecclesiastes, does not reflect the fuller revelation of the New Testament. The pessimistic view of life and death reveals what human eyes see which do not see beyond death's veil. Out of the fact that future destiny is in God's hands, grows the God-given expectation of divine judgment. What mortal cannot know about the future that God by revelation can and does make known? (Ecclesiastes 9:1-6) One does not sin with impurity. A life of self indulgence and self-chosen ways ultimately answers to God in judgment. God's judgment is thorough. He considers every deed, even the secret things. His judgment is fair. He considers both the good things and the evil. New Testament distinguishes judgment for the wicked and the good. It shows that the evil are punished and the good are rewarded (Ecclesiastes 12:14).

> "Woe to those who rise early in the morning to run after their drinks, who stay up late at night, til they are inflamed with wine. They have harps and lyres at their banquets, tambourines, flutes and wine, but they have no regard for the deeds of the Lord. No respect for the work of His hands (Isaiah 5:11-12)"

These verses pronounce judgment on those who have sought ultimate value for their lives in strong drink. Alcohol makes us forget what God has done for us and so distorts our moral perceptions. We do not realize that we stand under divine judgment.

Hypocritical worship calls down God's harshest judgment (Isaiah 29:13-14). The prophetic task involved opposing God's disobedient people and announcing historical judgment on them. God's word doe not proclaim false hope to an unfaithful people (Jeremiah 1:14-19). Even when people reject God, their life and its consequences bear witness to God's will and purposes. Judah's rejection forced God to use them as fuel for His revelation. They themselves fanned the flame of His will. People take great risk when they reject the prophetic word. God's word is never a lie. His word becomes a fire burning up those who reject it. The prophetic judgment speech paved the way for God's judging actions (Jeremiah 5:12-17). Judgment comes upon family when Fathers lead the family into idolatry. The Old Testament prophets described in graphic terms God's judgment upon the nation, including families when the people followed false gods instead of remaining faithful to their covenant with Him (Jeremiah 9:13-16).

Whoever dismisses the Lord's will from future plans, will soon run out of time (Ezekiel 7:1-27). An unjust people who think that they can fool God face His inevitable judgment (Ezekiel 9:9-10). The Law of Judgment is followed by the Gospel of Hope. God does not practice total destruction. He saves the remnant and gives them undivided commitment to Him. God does everything possible to create a people who will freely let Him be their God. Those serving other gods do not qualify for the elect remnant (Ezekiel 11:15). Israel heard so much preaching of judgment that they became skeptical. They refused to believe judgment would come in their generation. Ezekiel called for a turn away from skepticism. God would bring judgment immediately. Israel learned that God's word is true. God judges a disobedient people. Ignoring God's word does not allow one to escape the historical of the judgment He announces (Ezekiel 12:1-28). Preaching to win popularity or money cannot reverse the reality of God's judgment. Neither can magic or folk religion. God judges those who try to shield God's people from His word of wrath and judgment (Ezekiel 13:1-23). Judgment is not blind anger lashing out without reason. God's judgment, just as His deliverance, works to accomplish God's eternal purpose of forming a permanent relationship with a faithful people. He uses all elements of creation to judge His people – human armies, natural disaster, wild animals, and sickness (Ezekiel 14:2-23). God's judgment comes when His people are unfaithful to Him. Judgment reveals the divine nature and power of God to a people who have forgotten the lessons of God's deliverance (Ezekiel 15:6-8).

God's judgment on His people is not a rare occurrence. Its long history reaches back to the wilderness. His judgment is not a total destruction, but a purging of the rebels (Ezekiel 20:35-38). God is the eternal judge who holds records of each kingdom and individual. No one will be treated unfairly when He pronounces the ultimate decision. God's law extends beyond His chosen people to all humanity, making everyone accountable to Him. Judgment comes on all who break the moral standards obvious to all people. God's wrath is His judgment upon sin. No sinful nation or people can escape His wrath. All inhabitants of history stand under the basic moral laws God has built into history. Immoral unjust treatment of other people, lead to judgment. As often with the prophets, Amos pronounced judgment on foreign nations building hope for salvation for God's nation. Then Israel and Judah found themselves in the list of nations. Foreign to God and facing His judgment (Amos 1:3-2:16). Amos' strategy was to get Israel's attention by pronouncing God's judgment on Israel's neighbors. God's judgment is not partial. His call for righteousness is called on Israel, too. Justice is an ethical norm recognized by and expected of all nations. God's chosen people will be chosen for judgment if they stubbornly oppose God. When God's people become so depraved, they forget how to act rightly. They are ripe for God's discipline. False worship and greed rob people of moral sensitivity and make judgment necessary (Amos 3:1-14). Repent or perish summarizes the Bible's inspired message. Israel refused to repent. Then they had to prepare to meet God in judgment. God brings judgment on people and nations because they deserve it (Obadiah 8-14).

God recorded a history of an individual prophet to teach a lesson about universal history. People with power remain sinners facing God's judgment. God wants even our enemies to repent and find a relationship with Him apart from judgment. Jonah wanted to destroy the hated national enemy.

God wanted to save for His purposes the international power, seeing them in their innocence and need (Jonah 1:1-4:11). Sin is not limited to church matters. God pays attention to our business practices. Cheating our customers is sin. Forgetting truth and honesty to get rich never pays in the long run. God intervenes to judge business sin. God's mark in our business life brings ultimate destruction (Micah 6:9-1). Micah described family conflict during the troubled times of God's judgment on Israel's sinfulness. Family members could not trust each other (Micah 7:5-6). Judgment is meant to cleanse and purify. When judgment is complete, God restores a remnant of His people who have been refined in the fires of judgment. These people call on the name of the Lord as God intended (Zechariah 13:8-9). God's presence can be dangerous. People think they can hide their sins and never be convicted. God comes to witness against sinners: those who practice magic or perform sexual sins, who are liars, oppressors of the poor, and perpetrators of injustice. We do not want to face God as a witness against us in His court.

> "So I will come near to you for judgment. I will be quick to testify against sorcerers, adulterers and perjurers against those who defraud laborers of their wages, who oppress the widows and the fatherless, and deprave aliens of justice, but do not fear me, says the Lord Almighty." (Malachi 3:5)

God has elected to bring complete justice to pass only on the day of the Lord, when He will judge all wickedness and destroy it. For the faithful, that will be a day of blessing In it God will ultimately show He rules the world.

In the New Testament Gospel Jesus states:

> "But I say unto you, that whosoever is angry with his brother without a cause shall be in danger of judgment: and whosoever shall say to his brother, Raca, shall be in danger of the council: but whosoever shall say, Thou food, shall be in danger of hell fire." (Matthew 5:22)

A progression in describing possible punishment ended with the danger of hell. Jesus warned of the "Gehenna of Fire." The reference was apparently to the Valley of Hinnom (Nehemiah 11:30) outside Jerusalem where rubbish was burned. Sadly, the valley was remembered as the place where Manasseh (II Kings 21:6) and others had sacrificed children to Baal or Molech in the valley (II Kings 23:10; II Chronicles 28:3; 33:6; Jeremiah 2:23; 19:1-13; 32:35). The continual burning of Gehenna afforded a vivid image for the place of eternal torment. Drastic action is advised to avoid suffering in Gehenna. (Matthew 5:29-30; 18:9; Mark 9:43-47) Both the body and the soul are destroyed there (Matthew 10:28). It is home to religious hypocrites

(Matthew 23:15, 33). Go has the power to throw people into Gehenna (Luke 12:5). Hell finds expression through human speech (James 3:6). The Old Testament phrase, "the Day of the Lord", shortened to "that Day!" (Joel 2:38-32; Amos 5:18-20; Zephaniah 1:14-2:3) It refers to the future day of judgment for those whose lives bear evil fruit. It is the day when the faithful and genuine enter the future kingdom. "That Day" will be one of separation based on true character as revealed in outward conduct. Final judgment will depend on Jesus' word to the Father concerning each person. Total allegiances to Him and total commitment to His way of life are the criteria for judgment. "Eternal fire" and the "Fire of hell" are mentioned in parallel statements of warning. The punishment (fire) of hell is clearly of eternal duration. The primary concern of this text is dealing radically with sin in the lives of Jesus' followers. It is enforced by the almost incidental invoking of the danger of eternal punishment in hell. The matter of fact, employment of the fire of hell as motivation underscores its reality and seriousness (Matthew 18:8, 9). The point of Jesus is that God's final judgment will result in eternal separation between the righteous and the wicked. Final judgment will be based on what actual deeds reveal about the true inner spiritual state of persons, not what verbal professions may have claimed. Hypocrisy cannot survive the judgment. Final destiny for the unrighteous will be the company of the devil and his angels in everlasting fire separated from God forever. To be ashamed of Jesus and His words now will have serious consequences then. At the time of judgment, the son of man will be ashamed of such a one.

One principle of divine judgment will be fitted to variations of opportunity, thus to degrees of accountability. Premeditated on high-handed sins have always been deserving of greater punishment than unwitting sins (Luke 12:48; Numbers 15:22-31). The result of this principle is that there are to be degrees of punishment and reward. People who reject salvation in Jesus Christ face eternal separation from God in hell. There they will realize how vital it is to receive God's forgiveness and life. The rich man, even in hell, was so aware of these truths that he wanted someone to tell his brothers of the eternal fate of those who refuse Jesus Christ. The return of the son of man (Jesus), will interrupt daily routines unexpectedly. God came to us in the flesh in Jesus. Rejecting Jesus brings God's judgment on us. The final consummation (last days) is to be accompanied by a judgment upon the present world order out of the cosmic judgment will come the new redeemed order of nature and the world. The last days and their climactic catastrophes will be followed by the "great and glorious day of the Lord." (Acts 2:16-21')

Miracles can judge as well as healings. The greed of Ananias and Sapphire produced premeditated deception. This is a high-handed sin against the Holy Spirit. Peter himself did not pronounce judgment against Ananias. Ananias and Sapphire died, and the early church interpreted it as God's judgment on their deception. When families conspire together to deceive God and His people, they bring God's judgment on the individuals in the family (Acts 5:1-11). Opposition to God may bring a miracle of judgment. The Lord works in mysterious ways (Acts 12:23). God judges human beings according to their conduct. Divine judgment is an on-going reality in this present time. There are temporal judgments and punishments for evil. However, the "Day of God's Wrath" will be a future, final judgment. Evil conduct can cause a strong cup of divine wrath. God carries out judgment, both present and future, on the basis of underlying principles. Judgment will be on an individual basis; rather than a national one, as was often the case in the Old Testament. It will be conducted on the basis of works, as the true inner character is revealed through conduct.

Divine judgment will be without partiality. It will be based on the response to the knowledge and understanding of God that an individual has. Even the secrets of human hearts will be judged. God is righteous and will judge the world fairly. Humans are not authorized to judge others. The fact that all of us must stand before God's judgment-seat, is sobering. (Acts 14:10-12) God's mercy and power are able to keep us safe to fill us with triumphant joy on Judgment Day.

Back in the Old Testament history, God gave power to Kings to make judgments.

> "And all Israel heard of the judgment, which the King had judged; and they feared the King; for they saw that the wisdom of God was in him, to do justice (I Kings 3:28).

King Solomon's decision arrived at by his keen-sighted appeal to the instincts of human nature, his showed insight into the workings of the human heart. Men who judged must be wise and full of knowledge.

> "And I charged your judges at times, saying: Hear the causes between your brethren, and judge righteously between a man and his brother, and the stranger that is with him (Deuteronomy 1:16)."

Here between; not to listen to ex parte statements, but to all that is said on both sides. The matters involving equity, there must be no difference between an Israelite and the resident alien, you must never show partiality to any person in a case. The judge must avoid everything that can possibly be construed as a bribe. The judge should feel that he is God's representative, and that every judicial decision is a religious act.

"And the King said to the judge, consider what ye do,; for ye judge not for man, but for the Lord; and He is with you in the matter of judgment." (II Chronicles 19:6)

In Jewish teaching all those who administer the Law in accordance with right, and thereby maintain the moral foundations – truth and justice – upon which human society rests, are performing a divine task. Every judge who renders righteous judgment, scripture deems him a copartner of the Holy One, blessed be He, in the work of creation. Deuteronomy states:

"And we took all his cities at that time, and utterly destroyed every city, the men and the women, and the little ones; we left none remaining." (Deuteronomy 2:34)

Utterly destroyed, placed them under the ban of extermination. Such was the rule of warfare in the days of old, when war was a sacred act. The ruthlessness of those methods is as hideous to us today as war itself will – we hope and pray – be to the men and women of the future and if it is the wholesale nature of the destruction that especially shocks our moral judgment, it is well for us to consider that in the next world war it is especially the defenseless population that will exposed to annihilation. Righteousness is the principle of right action in individuals; judgment is the embodiment of that principle in judicial decisions. In the absence of every sign of repentance on the part of the perverse rules, one means only remains to bring about better conditions-the judgment. Through punishment of these rulers, God will vindicate His honour, and hasten the restoration in Zion. Both Zion and her children will be redeemed through the justice and righteousness which the regenerate people exhibit. Isaiah never lost hope that a part of the nation – a righteous remnant – would repent. That sanctified minority would survive the judgment, which would befall Israel, and become the seed of a holy, indestructible, eternal people; the judgments of the two ways (Deuteronomy 11:26-32). It is an earnest appeal that a right choice is made between the two ways now before Israel. The entire future of the nation depends upon the right choice. Both as individuals and as a nation were endowed with free-will, and the choice between the two ways rested with themselves.

Judges and Justice - Provision is to be made for an ordered civil government. Justice must be free, accessible and absolutely impartial (I Chronicles 19:5-11). Judges must be both competent and impartial, and are not to be appointed for social or family reasons. Malachi preaches to a despondent generation, when spiritual lassitude possessed both high and low, and doubt paralyzed the souls of men. Sordidness, callousness and moral disintegration met him at every turn: and at the same time men asked, where is God? Malachi answers the challenge by announcing the speedy advent of a great judgment day. An answer to the doubters who perplexed by the social wrongs about them, and the prosperity of evil doers asked, "Where is the God of judgment?" (Malachi 2:17) Judgment will not wait until witnesses are produced, for I, knowing all secrets, am witness as well as Judge. I the Lord change not . . . are not consumed. I change not in my nature, being ever the same both in loving good and hating evil as in the purpose for which you are selected as my people. Therefore, my judgment is but to purify you for the fulfillment of your destiny.

In the day that I do make (Malachi 3:17) - The Day of Judgment. The faithful minority will be safe. They will be God's own possession and treasure.

The great and terrible day – of judgment announced in the preceding chapter terrible in the sense of awesome.

He shall turn the heart – the heart was considered the seat of thought as well as emotion.

At every turn of your life, keep the end in view; remember that you will have to stand before a strict judge, who knows everything, who cannot be won over by gifts or talked around by excuses, and who will give you your deserts. What sort of defense will you make before one who knows the worst that can be said against you – poor, sinful fool, so often panic-stricken when you meet with human disapproval. Strange, that you should look forward so little to the Day of Judgment, when there will be no counsel to plead for you, because everyone will be hard put to it, to maintain his own cause. Now is the time to work, while there is a harvest to be reaped; now is the time when tears and sighs and lamenting of you will be taken into account and listened to, and can make satisfaction for the debt you owe. Nothing so important, nothing so useful, if you want to clear your soul of that debt, is to be a man who can put up with great deal. Such a man, if he is wronged is more distressed over the sin committed than over the wrong done him; he is always ready to say a prayer for his enemies, forgives an injury with all his heart and is quick to ask forgiveness of others, and you will find him more easily moved to pity than to anger. And all the while, he is putting constraints upon himself, doing all he can to make corrupt nature the servant of the spirit. Much better to get rid of your sins now, prune away your bad habits here, than keep them to be paid for hereafter; it's only our preposterous attachment to creature comforts that blind us. Those fires; what is it they will feed on, but your sins? The more you spare yourself and take corrupt nature for your guide, the heavier price you will pay later on, the more fuel you are storing up for those fires. The pattern of a man's sins will be the pattern of his punishment. Red-hot goads to spur on the idle, cruel hunger and thirst to torment the glutton; see where the dissipated souls, that so loved their own pleasures, are bathed in hot pitch and reeking sulphur where the envious souls go howling like mad dogs, for every grief. Each darling sin will find its appropriate reward, for the proud, every kind of humiliation, for the covetous and the pinch of grinding poverty. Spend a hundred years of penance here on earth, would be no match for one hour of that punishment. Here we have intervals of rest, and our friends can comfort us; there is no respite for the damned, no consolation for the damned. Take your sins seriously now, be sorry for them now, and at the Day of Judgment you will have the confidence; the confidence of blessed souls. How fearlessly then, the just will confront those persecutors of theirs, who kept them down all the time. The man who submitted to human judgments so meekly will now take rank as judge; in perfect calm they will stand there, the poor, the humble, while the proud are daunted by every prospect that meet them. A well-disciplined life of hard penitential exercise, not a good time here on earth, will be your choice then.

You have got to realize that all your sufferings here are slight ones, and will set you off much worse sufferings hereafter. How much will you be able to stand there? The amount you can stand here is a good test. You, who find it so hard to bear these pin-pricks, how will you be able to take eternal punishment? What will you make of hell; when you make such a-to do about small discomforts? No, you can't have your own way twice over; you can't take your pleasures in this world and then reign with Christ. And now, suppose you had lived all your life, and were still living today, surrounded with honors and pleasures; what use would it all be, if you were to fall down dead this instant? Everything, you see, is just meaningless, except loving God and giving all our loyalty to Him. Love God with all your heart and you've nothing to fear. Death or punishment, judgment or hell; love, when it reaches its full growth, is an unfailing passport to God's presence. If we are still harkening over our sinful habits, of course we are afraid of death and judgment. Just as well, all the same, that if love can't succeed in beckoning us away from evil courses, we should be scared away by the fear of hell. Only, if a man doesn't make the fear of God his first consideration, his good resolutions won't last. He will walk into some trap of the devil's before long.

# CHAPTER II
# THE JUDGMENT ON ADAM,
# EVE AND THE SERPENT

When God created man, He gave man free will to do as he pleases. Man used his free will to disobey God's command and because of that, man's freedom was on trial. God call out to Adam (the man) and summoned him to the witness stand. "Where art thou?" is the call which after every sin resounds in the ears of the man who seeks to deceive himself and others concerning his sin. Adam's (the man) answer was, "I hide because I was naked." Notice that one sin leads to another sin. Adam (the man) commits a further offence by attempting to conceal the truth by means of this excuse. There are no excuses for sinning. God gave Adam (the man) an opportunity for full confession and expression of contrition. A sin un-confessed and un-repented is a sin constantly committed. Finding his excuse useless, Adam (the man) throws the blame upon everybody, but himself. First of all it is Eve (the woman); then he insolently fixes a share of the responsibility upon God – "Whom thou gavest to be with me."

> "God said, unto Adam, because thou hast harkened unto the voice of thy wife, and hast eaten of the tree, of which I commanded thee saying; thou shalt not eat of it: cursed is the ground for thy sake; in toil shalt thou eat of it all the days of thy life." (Genesis 3:17)

It was Adam's duty from the beginning to till the ground (Genesis 2:15), but the work would now become much more laborious. The soil would henceforth yield its produce only as the result of hard and uncasing toil. "Thou shalt eat the herb," render, whereas thou eatest the herb of the field. The spontaneous growth of the soil will be weeds which are unsuitable for human consumption. Man's food is the herb, which he can only acquire by toil.

> "In the sweat of thy face shalt thou eat bread, till thou return unto the ground: For out of it wast thou taken: For dust thou art, and unto dust shalt thou return." (Genesis 3:19)

The necessity of labour has proved man's greatest blessing and has been the cause of all progress and improvement. Man was put out of the Garden of Eden, "because man has become as one of us", said God. As one of the angels: or "us", is a plural of majesty (Genesis 1:26), meaning man is become as God – Omniscient. Man, having through disobedience secured the faculty of unlimited knowledge, there was real danger that his knowledge would outstrip his sense of obedience to Divine Law.

> "Lest he put forth his hand, and take also of the tree of life, and eat, and live forever." (Genesis 3:22)

Through further disobedience, he could secure deathlessness. Immortality, however, that had been secured through disobedience and lived in sin, an immortal life of intellect without conscience would defeat the purpose of man's creation. Therefore, not only for his punishment, but for his salvation to bring him back from the sinister course in which he had entered, God sent man forth from the Garden. Man, having sunk into sin, must rise again through the spiritual purification of suffering and death. Sin drives men from God's presence; and when man banishes God from his world, he dwells in a wilderness instead of a Garden of Eden. The man was forbidden to enter the Garden again, and the slightest attempt on his part to do so would bring down upon him instant destruction. (Genesis 3:24)

The work itself was not the punishment for sin. Rather, the difficult, frustrating, and unremitting toil which comes from dealing with an unresponsive environment because the lot of humanity. The unrelieved nature of this kind of labor led ultimately to the grave, re-emphasizing human mortality.

> "Unto the woman He said: I will greatly multiply thy pain and thy travail; in pain thou shalt bring forth children; and thy desire shall be to thy husband, and he shall rule over thee." (Genesis 2:16-17)

Greatly multiply . . . over thee. Better, much, much will I make thy pain and thy travail; in pain wilt thou bring forth children, and thy desire is unto thy husband and he ruleth over thee. This is no sentence upon the woman.

It does not contain the word "cursed." Moreover, God Himself pronounced the fruitfulness of man a blessing (Genesis 1:28), and therewith woman's pain and travail are inextricably bound up, being part of woman's physical being. The words addressed to the woman are therefore parenthetical, and signify in effect: "Thee I need not punish." A sufficiency of woe and suffering is thine because of thy physical being. The desire, in spite of the pains of travail and the longing for motherhood, remains the most powerful instinct in woman.

In this passage, female subordination is introduced into the one flesh relationship that previously (Genesis 1-2) had heed one shared authority over physical world. The judgment on Eve included increased pain in childbearing and subordination, if you want to call this a judgment, to the husband for whom she has desire that leads to childbearing. Since Eve had not yet given birth, this judgment explained the pain associated with the joy of becoming a mother. The condition that her sexual desire be for her husband alone influenced some interpreters to propose that sexuality was in some way involved in the "fall." This idea is probable that this condition is related to the previous one on childbearing. Even though childbirth is associated with pain and pregnancy as the result of sexual union, the wife is to continue to desire sexual relations with her husband. Since Eve had refused to obey God's instructions given through Adam, he was to rule over her. Such subordination was not in the original purpose of God for marriage, but is a consequence to Eve's failure to obey God.

> "And the Lord God said unto the serpent: because thou hast done this, cursed art thou from among all cattle, and from among all beasts of the field; upon thy belly shalt thou go, and dust shalt thou eat all the days of thy life." (Geneses 3:14)

The serpent, as the tempter and instigator of the offence, sentence is passed upon it first; and as the tempter, the Serpent is cursed and not its dupes and victims. Upon thy belly thou goest and dust thou eatest. Till the eighteenth century, it was the general belief that the serpent had been walking upright and was now reduced to crawling. This is quite un-biblical. The meaning is, continue to crawl on thy belly and eat dust. Henceforth, it will be regarded as a curse, recalling to men thy attempt to drag them to the dust all the days of thy life, as long as thy species lasts.

# CHAPTER III
# THE JUDGMENT ON CAIN

The words spoken by Eve are very obscure:

> "And the man knew Eve his wife; and she conceived and bore Cain
> and said, "I have gotten a man with the help of the Lord.""

The traditional interpretation makes 'a man' refer to Cain; and the
words, an expression of thanksgiving for her child. The sequel to the act
of disobedience in the Garden would have caused estrangement between
husband and wife; and Eve rejoices in the birth of a child, because through
Cain, she wins back her husband. The traditional interpretation reference
(Genesis 29:32). Cain had a younger brother, his name was Abel. Abel is given
the lighter task of caring for the flocks; while Cain assists his Father in the
cultivation of the soil.

> "And in process of time is come to pass, that Cain brought of the
> fruit of the ground an offering unto the Lord."

An Offering – this is the first mention of worship in scripture. The religious
instinct is part of man's nature, and sacrifice is the earliest outward expression
of that worship. Its purpose was to express acknowledgment of his bounty to
the given of all.

> "And shalt he also brought of the <u>firstlings</u> of his flock and of the
> <u>fat</u> thereof."

<u>Firstlings</u> – the most highly prized among the flocks.

The Fat – the richest part of the animal.
Had respect unto – accepted.

"But unto Cain and to his offering, He had not respect."

But unto Cain – unlike Abel's sacrifice, his sacrifice is rejected because of the difference of spirit in which it was offered. The Lord looks to the heart.
His countenance fell – in disappointment and rejection.

"If thou doest well, shall it not be lifted up? And if doest not well, sin croucheth at the door; and unto thee is its desire, but thou mayest rule over it."

Shall it not be lifted up? – alluding to the 'countenance' that had fallen. God mercifully intervenes to arrest the progress of evil thoughts. Another interpretation is, shall there not be acceptance?
Sin croucheth – sin is compared to a ravenous beast lying in wait for its prey. It crouches at the entrance of the house, to spring upon its victim as soon as the door opens. By harboring feelings of vexation, Can opened the door of his heart to the evil passions of envy, anger and violence which eventually ended in murder.
And unto thee – passion and evil imaginations are ever assaulting the heart of man; yet, he can conquer them if only he resist them with determination.

"And Cain spoke unto Abel his brother, 'Let's go into the field.' And it came to pass when they were in the field, that Cain rose up against Abel his brother, and slew him." (Genesis 4:8)

In the field – far away from their parent's home, where Cain had his brother at his mercy. (Deuteronomy 22:25) In slaying Abel, Cain slew also Abel's unborn descendents. He who destroys a single human life is as if he destroyed a whole world.

### The Sentence

"And now cursed art thou from the ground, which hath opened her mouth to receive thy brother's blood from thy hand. When thou tillest the ground, it shall not henceforth yield unto thee her strength; a fugitive and a wonderer shalt thou be in the earth.'(Genesis 4:11, 12)

More than the ground, upon which a curse had been pronounced (Genesis 3:17). Wherever he lives, the curse will follow him and the soil will be barren for him. The remainder of his existence will consequently be an unceasing vagabondage.

Cain was the first person born on earth, the oldest son of Adam and Eve. He was the first murderer. Why? Because of the jealousy for his brother, he opposed him and finally took his life even after the Lord had warned him about his jealousy and his sin (Genesis 4:6, 7). Cain did not love the Lord, as we know, not only from his deeds, but also from the attitude of his heart in offering to the Lord (Genesis 4:5). The Lord cursed Cain for his fratricide so that he became a fugitive and wonderer. The earth he tilled would no longer yield to him its strength (Genesis 4:11, 12).

Each person born develops individual characteristics and personalities. Cain turned out to be a bad boy. His jealousy and anger determined his decision to kill his brother. These sinful emotions erupted when God accepted Abel's sacrifice but did not look with favor upon Cain's. He had to bear responsibility for his sinful deeds (jealousy and anger). God gave Cain a chance to repent or confess, "If you do what is right." God indicated to Cain what he needed to do to make his gift acceptable, but Cain refused God's advise. His jealousy and anger wouldn't let him. "Cain went out from the presence of the Lord, and dwelt in the Land of Nod, on the east of Eden." (Genesis 4:16) Having forfeited God's favour, Cain withdraws from the neighborhood of Eden, which was the special abode of the Divine Presence.

# CHAPTER IV
# THE JUDGMENT OF THE WORLD
# IN THE DAYS OF NOAH

"And the earth was corrupt before God, and the earth was filled with violence. And God saw the earth, and behold it was corrupt; for all flesh had corrupted their way upon the earth. And God said unto Noah; the end of all flesh is come before me; for the earth is filled with violence through them; and behold, I will destroy them with the earth." (Genesis 6:11-13)

These are the scriptures that explain the reason for the judgment of the world in Noah's days. The inhabitants of the earth were filled with gross immorality. What they did was an offence in the sight of God. All flesh, including the animals. Their corruption manifested itself in the development of ferocity.

### Make Thee An Ark

The Ark was to be prepared for the coming judgment. The construction of the Ark occupied Noah for 120 years, in order to give his contemporaries an opportunity to repent. Their curiosity would naturally be aroused by their enquiring by warning them of the judgment which God was bringing on mankind.

"And I, behold, I do bring the flood of waters upon the earth to destroy all flesh, wherein is the breath of life from under heaven; everything that is in the earth shall perish." (Genesis 6:17)

These emphatic words bring out the thought of the terrible necessity of the flood. Because of Noah's righteousness, God made a covenant with Noah. God will fulfill His promise to spare Noah and his family.

## The Start of the Judgment

"In the six hundredth year of Noah's life, in the second month, on the seventeenth day of the month, on the same day were all the fountains of the great deep broken up, and the windows of heaven were opened. And the rain was upon the earth forty days and forty nights." (Genesis 7:11-12)

There was a seismic upheaval; the earth was swept by a gigantic tidal wave, and simultaneously there was a torrential downpour of rain.

Windows of heaven – for the expression; II Kings 7:2, 19; Malichi 3:10; as if the last reservoirs of water thought of as stored above the sky were coming down through special openings, constantly and in resistless strength.

There was heavy rain. A continued down pour for the period of time specified. After it had rained for forty days, the waters were sufficiently deep to bear the Ark which had previously been like a heavily-laden ship stuck in shallow water and unable to move. The waters covered the earth. It will be noted that there were three stages in the increase of the waters. The first was marked by the lifting of the Ark (Genesis 7:17); the second by the floating of the Ark (Genesis 7:18); and the third by the total submergence of the mountains (Genesis 7:19). The waters were 22 ½ (twenty-two and a half) feet above the top of the highest mountain.

"And all flesh perished that moved upon the earth, both fowl, and cattle, and beast, and every swarming thing that swarmeth upon the earth, and every man; all in whose nostrils was the breath of the spirit of life, whatsoever was in the dry land, died. And He blotted out every living substance which was upon the face of the ground, both man and cattle and creeping thing, and fowl of the heaven; and they were blotted out from the earth; and Noah only was left, and they that were with him in the Ark. (Genesis 7:21-23)

The waters dominated the earth. After forty days of down pour, the waters reached their highest point and remained so for a period of one hundred and ten days. After 150 days had passed from the commencement of the flood, the waters began to diminish. This is the judgment on the land (world) in Noah's days. In the future, God will punish the individual sinners, and not the human family as a body.

# CHAPTER V
# THE JUDGMENT ON BABEL

". . . the whole earth was of one language and of one speech."
(Genesis 11:1)

They had but a small vocabulary. The territory of Babylon consisted of an almost unbroken plain in Shinar, and they dwelt there. It is more and more coming to be regarded as the cradle of the earliest civilization.

"And they said: come, let us build us a city, and a tower, with its top in heaven, and let us make us a name; lest we be scattered abroad upon the face of the whole earth." (Genesis 11:4)

God wanted them to be scattered to go and replenish the earth.

With its top in heaven – an exaggerated statement (Deuteronomy 1:28); the cities are great and walled up to heaven.
Let us make us a name – if they all dwelt together, they would be powerful and become renowned.

"And the Lord came down to see the city and the tower, which the children of men builded." (Genesis 11:5)

Came down to see – rule that a judge should never condemn an offender, without first seeing for himself, both him and the nature of the offence.

At this early stage in human history, men are led to combine by an unworthy motive. If their design is not frustrated, they might employ their united strength for outrageous purpose. All human effort is both futile and empty, if dictated by self-exaltation and divorced from acknowledgment of God.

Babel – This is an instance of popular etymology based on resemblance of sound and is frequently found in scripture. The Assyrian name for Babel means, "Gate of God."

One explanation of Genesis, chapter 11 is that is continues the theme of the preceding section and indicates that the divine ideal was one humanity united by one universal language. In view of the division of mankind by diversity of tongue, which has ever been a source of misunderstanding, hostility and war, this chapter answers the question how the original Divinely ordained unity of language, that indispensable link for the unity of mankind, was lost. Only a great transgression - an enterprise colossal in its insolent impiety and evidencing an open revolt against God – could account for such a moral catastrophe to humanity (Steinthal). Hebrews' minds were the ziggurats, the Mesopotamian Temple – towers, rising to an immense height as if intended to scale Heaven.

The building of the greatest of these towers was associated with Babylon, the centre of ancient luxury and power. The Rabbis assert that the builders of this Tower of Babel wished to storm the heaven in order to wage war against the Deity; and as the highest stage in an Assyrian or Babylonian ziggurat was surmounted by a shrine of the Deity, there is perhaps less fancifulness in these words than is often suspected.

Quite a different interpretation of this chapter is given by Ibn Ezra: the purpose of the builders was simply to prevent their becoming separated, and to secure their dwelling together. But as this purpose was contrary to the design of providence (9:1; 1, 28) that the whole earth should be inhabited, it was frustrated. The expression whose top may reach unto heaven must accordingly be interpreted that, that tower was to be of very great height so that is would be visible at a considerable distance and become a rallying point to all people.

God did not intend for a major part of the world to remain uninhabited. Human pride and arrogance produced the Tower of Babel. God responded in limited judgment. He scattered the human population throughout the earth and brought about the diversity of human languages. This miraculous judgment created a new human situation demanding a new stage in God's missionary work to redeem all people. God's own estimate of human potentiality is one of the highest compliments paid to humankind anywhere in the Bible (Genesis

11:6). Cooperative efforts which are unified and unrestricted can have almost unlimited results. The attainments of the age of Babel bear testimony of a highly advanced technology. God created humans to have fellowship with Him, and enjoy the privileges of serving their creator. Instead, people chose to serve their own pride and egotism. Rather than trusting God to protect them and preserve their community, they took matters in their own hands. Rebellion against God on the individual or community level is sin. We are called to trust God, not to usurp His place.

Man finds ways to praise his own glory. Right after the flood, mankind proposed to build in the Land of Shinar, a tower reaching unto heaven (Genesis 11:1-9). The intention was on the one hand to create a mighty monument for their own glory and fame, "Let us make a name."; and on the other hand to establish a central dwelling place for concentrated power, "Lest we be scattered abroad upon the face of the whole earth." However, God drastically ended this proud attempt by the confusion of tongues. The Land of Shinar is to be identified with Babylon, for Genesis 10:10 lists the cities in the Land of Shinar as Babel, Erech, Accad and Calneh; and these were all cities in the Land of Babylon. (Genesis 11:9)

# CHAPTER VI
# THE JUDGMENT OF SODOM AND GOMORRAH

The destruction of Sodom ranks among the most wonderful events in Bible history. In the original narrative and in every subsequent allusion made to it in scripture, it is described as miraculous. The sin of the people became so great, so abominate, so universal that even divine mercy could no longer suffer it to pollute the earth-a mercy that would have spared the whole guilty pent-polis had only ten righteous men been found therein. Sulphur and fire were rained upon the cities (Sodom and Gomorrah) and the plain from heaven. The destructive power of these agencies was doubtlessly and greatly increased by the bitumen which was so abundant in the surrounding region. It was a fiery destruction, and the Bible nowhere takes cognizance of any other element. The cities were totally consumed, and their ruin was feral. In fact, the destruction of Sodom and other cities of the plain was so terrible and so complete that it was taken in all subsequent ages as the type of utter and everlasting ruin.,

"As in the overthrow of Sodom and Gomorrah, and the neighbor cites thereof, said the Lord, no man shall abide there, neither shall a son of man dwell on it." (Jeremiah 49:18)

Before the judgment of destruction, God sent three angels to visit those wicked cities:

(1) One to announce the tidings of the birth of Israel;
(2) The second to destroy Sodom and Gomorrah; and
(3) The third to rescue Lot.

An angel is never sent on more than one errand at a time.

The cry of Sodom and Gomorrah – the cries of those who suffered from the atrocious wickedness of the inhabitants of Sodom and who implored Heaven's vengeance against their cruel oppressors (Ezekiel 16:49). The following legend graphically describes their hatred of all strangers and their fiendish punishment of all who departed from their ways.

A girl overcome by pity, supplied food to a poor stranger. On detection, she was stripped, bound, daubed with honey and placed on the roof under the burning sun to be devoured by bees.

Their sin is exceeding grievous. – As in the days of Noah.

> I will go down now. – An anthropomorphic expression, as in Genesis 11:7, to convey the idea that before God decided to punish the dwellers of the cities, He descended as it were, to obtain ocular proof of or extenuating circumstances for their crimes.

Abraham's plea for Sodom and Gomorrah is a single illustration of his nobility of character. Amid the hatreds and feuds of primitive tribes who glorified brute force and despised pity, Abraham proves true to his new name and embraces in his sympathy all the children of men. Even the wicked inhabitants of Sodom were his brothers, and his heart overflows with sorrow over their doom. The unique dialogue between God and Abraham teaches two vital lessons; first, the supreme value of righteousness and secondly, God's readiness for pardon (Ezekiel 28:11), if only He can do so consistently with justice.

Abraham rests his case on the conviction that the action of God cannot be arbitrary but only in accordance with perfect justice. In an indiscriminate destruction, however, all the inhabitants whether good or wicked, would share the same fate. Abraham pleads that as it would not be just to destroy the righteous, therefore, in order to save the righteous, the judgment which had been pronounced over the cities should be stayed. This intercession on behalf of Sodom and Gomorrah-Abraham arguing with God, yea, bargaining with Him, to save their depraved inhabitants from merited destruction – is the highest spiritual pinnacle reached by the patriarch.

When Abraham could not find fifty righteous men in Sodom, and pleaded on behalf of forty, thirty, twenty, ten that the great city might be spared, do you think God did not know all the time that there were not even ten righteous men in Sodom? Lot's wife did not escape the judgment, because she looked back and lingered behind, to be overtaken by the brimstone and fire from which the others escaped (Lot and his two daughters).

Judgment is a part of God's history, for humans do not consistently cooperate to achieve God's purpose. Judgment occurs in communication with God's faithful people and in mercy. In historical judgment, God's people see the Holy, righteous and just side of God's character. God's justice destroyed the wicked cities to protect His chosen people. God's wrath comes in judgment upon those who do not repent of their sins and turn to Him. How soon that judgment comes and how that wrath is expressed is not for us to determine. God's judgment came dramatically and decisively on Sodom and Gomorrah. God's grace often delays the exercise of His wrath to let His grace achieve positive results.

God attempts through His grace and His wrath to bring people to repentance, faith and responsible action. Wrath is God's last resort. Sin had engulfed Sodom and Gomorrah. God responded in miraculous judgment. Only Lot and his two daughters escaped the destruction of the two cities. Lot's greedy choice threatened the future of his whole people. In allowing him to escape, God preserved an entire nation. Living in a sinful environment does not justify deception. Nor does it justify expecting God to save us from the consequences of our sin. God may act to achieve His purposes, but he is not bound to act just because we claim to be His people. Just as God told Lot and his family to come out from the sinful environment, so the Apostle Paul stated, to come out from among them and be separated. (II Corinthians 6:17)

Lot seemed as though he did not want to leave. The Bible said he lingered. Either to collect his valuables, or he was reluctant to leave. All that scripture tells of Lot is characteristics of a weak, irresolute character.

# CHAPTER VII
# THE JUDGMENT OF PHAROAH
(Egypt and the Ten Plagues)

Pharaoh too, is a child of God, but a rebellious son (Deuteronomy 21:18), who must be chastised before he would let his bondmen go free.

The plagues are disciplinary chastisements of God. Instead of annihilating the tyrant by one mighty stroke, God, in His divine forbearance, inflicted ten successive plagues to break his pride. God warned Pharaoh ten times and ten times gave him respite to repent, and before punishing him. He - ten times – showed him His mercy. For there is grace and merciful forgiveness for those who repent; but, there is unsparing punishment for those, who, hardening their hearts to the voice of God, continue to oppress their fellowmen.

The ten plagues form a symmetrical and regularly unfolding scheme. The first nine plagues consist of three series of three each:

(1)  Blood, frogs, gnats
(2)  Fleas, murrain, boils
(3)  Hail, locusts, darkness

In each series the first plague is announced to Pharaoh beforehand at the brink of the Nile, the second is proclaimed by Moses at the Palace, and the third is sent without warning. Each series of plagues rises to a climax; the final series is the climax of all that preceded and these are but the prelude to the tenth plague – the death of the firstborn, which seals the completeness of the whole.

The first nine plagues, though often spoken of as wonders, are not fantastic miracles without any basis in natural phenomena. As everywhere else in scripture, the supernatural is here interwoven with the natural; and the plagues are but miraculously intensified forms of the diseases and other natural occurrences to which Egypt is more or less liable. Between June and August, the Nile usually turns to a dark red, owing to the presence vegetable matter. Generally after this time, the slime of the river breeds a vast number of frogs; and the air is filled with swarms of tormenting insects. We can therefore understand, that an exceptional defilement of the Nile would vastly increase the frogs which swarm in its waters that the huge heaps of decaying frogs would inevitably breed great swarms of flies, which in turn, would spread the disease-germs that attacked the animals and flocks in the pest-ridden region of the Nile. But, whether we place the greater emphasis on the natural or on the supernatural in the account of the plagues, we must never forget the purpose for which they were recorded. The purpose is not so much to give an exhaustive archeological or even historical chronicle, as it is a moral and religious instruction. The story of the plagues is drawn with unfading colors and its typical, didactic significance cannot be overrated. It depicts the impotence of man's strongest determination when it essays to contend with God, and the fruitfulness of all human efforts to frustrate His purpose.

The contest was for more than a dramatic humiliation of the unrepentant and infatuated tyrant. It was nothing less than a judgment on the gods of Egypt. The plagues fell on the principal divinities that were worshipped since times immemorial in the Nile Valley. The river was a god; it became loathsome to its worshippers. The frog was reiterated as the sign of fruitfulness, and it was turned into a horror. The cattle, the sacred ram, the sacred goat, and the sacred bull were all smitten. The sacred beetle became a torment to those who put their trust in its divinity. When we add to these the plague of darkness, which showed the eclipse of ra, the sun-god, we see that we have her a contrast between the God of Israel, the Lord of the universe, and the senseless idols of a senile civilization; as it is written (Exodus 12:12), "Against all the gods of Egypt, I will execute judgment: I am the Lord."

## The First Plague: The Water Turned Into Blood

Pharaoh goes out to the water to offer worship to the god of the river. The Nile, as the source of Egypt's fertility, was venerated under various names and symbols. In honor of the Nile god, religious festivals were held, at which Pharaoh himself sometimes officiated.

The plague spoke its own message; at the sight of the bloody Nile, the Egyptians were with horror reminded of Pharaoh's murderous command against the Hebrew children. The Nile possesses abundant fish, whose death

31

would be a national calamity, as fish was one of the principal articles of food in ancient Egypt.

<u>Loath to drink water</u> - they will exert themselves in vain to find a remedy to make the water of the Nile palatable. The arms of the Nile flow into the Mediterranean. The Nile has no tributary rivers.
<u>Streams</u> - Dug by human hands from the Nile to fertilize the fields.
<u>Pools</u> - Caused by the inundation of the Nile. (Isaiah 42:15)
<u>Ponds</u> – Wells, cisterns and reservoirs.
<u>In like manner</u> – From where did the magicians obtain water for their experiment, as all the water had been turned into blood? The magician took rain, or they obtained the water from Goshen, or they dug for it. Because of the magicians making an apparent change of small quantities of water into blood, which was one of the common tricks of Egyptian magic, Pharaoh, therefore, disregarding the universality and completeness of Moses' miracle, thought it nothing more than what he had often seen done by his magicians.

## The Second Plague: Frogs

This plague, like the preceding, was in general accordance with natural phenomena, but marvelous both for its extent and intensity. The extreme cleanliness of the Egyptians rendered this plague peculiarly disagreeable to them. Pharaoh acknowledges that this plague had been sent by the God of the Hebrews.

<u>In the river only</u> – where they would naturally be at any time. They departed from the houses, the bed-chambers, and the bed (sleeping with frogs!), frogs in the ovens, and into the kneading-troughs. It was frogs everywhere. Can you believe that after all those frogs, Pharaoh acknowledged that this plague had been sent by God, but he still once again hardened his heart. Again he breaks his promise when the Hebrew demanded the promised freedom.

## The Third Plague: Gnats

<u>Gnats</u> – sand flies, or fleas.
<u>Dust of the earth became gnats</u> – It appeared to the people, owing to the multitude of the insects.

"And the magicians did so with their secret outs to bring Forth gnats, but they could not; and there were gnats upon man, and upon beast. Then, the magicians said unto Pharaoh; "<u>This is the finger of</u>

God", and Pharaoh's heart was hardened, and the Lord had spoken."
(Exodus 8:14,15)

Finger of God – The magicians had encouraged Pharaoh in his defiance of
the divine will; their confessed failure now is more complete. They discern
the hands on work of God in the plague. To a certain extent, the magicians –
though they initiate nothing, and do not seem ever to have thought of reprisals
or counter plagues against Moses, or the Israelites – bring about by their
enchantments the same results as Moses and Aaron, although they only by
such means increase the calamity upon themselves. But after the second
plague, their power entirely ceases, and they suffer from the following disasters
quite like fellow countrymen.

The Israelites seem to have been involved in the first three plagues in
common with the Egyptians. These two circumstances along with this other,
that the initiatory sign, and even the first few plagues, were directed against
the eternal accessories of life, and not against life itself, though they may
to some extent have neutralized the immediate convincing effect of these
inflictions, yet have a high moral significance. The fact that the Israelites were
first involved and afterwards sacredly separated, taught them that they were
no less liable in themselves to the judgments of heaven than the nations; and
that being sinful, and indeed too great an extent involved in the sins of Egypt.
They must, but for God's mercy, be involved in her plagues.

The other circumstance, that the plagues were light at first, and proceeded
by slow degrees to terrible severity, and that they were not for a long time so
fearful as to compel submission, and not exclusively directed against the
Egyptians, shows that God desires to bring about His purposes, not by the
use of mere stupendous portent, but by appeals to the principles of truth and
justice that role in the breasts even of the heathen. God's wonders in Egypt
were clear enough at first to command reasonable recognition; and mercifully
arranged so that the Egyptians might on the occurrence of the preliminary
sign and at every successive plague, have let the people go, without themselves
suffering such terrible destruction.

The plagues seemed designed to show God's grasp of all the elements of
life and power in Egypt, and all the elements of destruction and death both
in it and beyond it, and His intention to wield all these for the humiliation of
that land and the deliverance of His people. So, that as the plagues advanced,
they more and more diverged into two distinct lines of operation:

(1) Proving with increasing clearness God's preponderance over the
    powers of Egypt; and
(2) Drawing wider the distinction between Egypt and Israel.

<u>Pharaoh sent.</u> – to see if it was even so; but the very knowledge embittered his heart the more.

### The Fourth Plague: Beetles

<u>Swarms of flies.</u> – Hebrew, ha-arob, a collective singular from a root meaning to mix.
<u>Beetles</u> – the beetle was sacred and was regarded as the emblem of the sun-god. It was sculptured on monuments, painted on tombs, engraved on gems, worn around the neck as an amulet and honored in ten thousand images.

> ". . . and there came grievous swarms of flies in the house of Pharaoh,
> and into his servants' houses; and in all the land of Egypt. The land
> was ruined by reason of the swarm of flies." (Exodus 8:20)

<u>Grievous</u> – burdensome, severe, numerous.
<u>The land was ruined</u> – not only did the Egyptians and their cattle suffer, but the daily occupations of the people were interrupted.

The first group of plagues – one to four inclusive; the chief source of life in Egypt is the Nile, the quicken of all growth by its annual overflow, filtered away into thousands of life-giving streams, drunk with avidity, worshipped with wildest fanaticism – the god and life – given of the country, as in all heathenism the sources of life are elevated to the rank of gods. The very fountain of the teeming life of the country - the first stoke falls; turning the water into blood under the first plague, and bringing loathsome reptiles from whence only food and fertility had before issued under the second. All this could not but show that the quickening power of the river die, not lie in itself, but that its life-giving energy was bestowed by a living God, who could take it away and turn it into death. Then the next two plagues – the gnats arising out of the fine dust of the land, and the flies bred upon the banks of the countless canals for irrigation – must be regarded as but a continuation of the same plague, pursuing the great god of the land through every ramification of His influence for the fine powered soil is that left after the inundation; and the canals and marshy swamps, which sent forth such countless armies of tormenters, are but the underlying vessels of the great central heart which throbbed its seems of life through all the members of the land. There is, however, an advance on two first plagues. In them the curse was upon and from the waters alone. In these two, it is from the productive soil and the irrigating streams – mixture of land and water.

In the next group, which embraces the three following plagues, a marked change takes place. Except in the Nile, life had not been directly assailed; only the productive powers of nature, too readily deems gods by the idolatrous Egyptians, had been smitten and made sources of misery to their former worshippers.

## The Fifth Plague: The Murrain on Cattle

A very grievous murrain – a rinderpest (Exodus 9:15)

> "And the Lord shall make a division between the cattle of Israel and the cattle of Egypt; and there shall nothing die of all that belongeth to the children of Israel." (Exodus 9:40)

The land of Goshen is again to be immune from the plague. God did not pour out His divine judgments on His children while pouring His divine judgment on the sinful nations. In the fifth plague the cattle die.

## The Sixth Plague: Boils

Small dust – the disease would be carried through Egypt by the air.

The magicians could not stand. Not only were they unable to imitate it, but they were themselves included in the affliction. Pharaoh's sin preceded and provoked God's punishments, which, however, for from moving his stubborn heart, intended to harden it still more and to bring him into a self-conscious opposition to the God of Israel.

To show thee my power – to make thee experience my power, which might have had the effect of softening Pharaoh's heart, and did in fact lead him more than once to give God the glory.

## The Seventh Plague: Hail

Exaltest thou thyself – thou raisest thyself as an obstacle against my people, and opposes their emancipation (Thou treadest down [oppresses] my people.)

> "And the Lord said unto Moses, stretch forth thy hand toward heaven, that there may be hail in all the land of Egypt, upon man, and upon beast, and upon every herb of the field, throughout the land of Egypt." (Exodus 19:22)

Upon man, and upon beast – of those who disregarded the divine warning.

Feared the word of the Lord – this is the first indication that the warnings had a salutary effect upon the Egyptians. (Exodus 9:20)

In the sixth plague, men and beasts are tormented with boils from the dust of the furnaces. In the seventh plague men, cattle and crops are struck down by the hail. First, cattle perished, but the people are untouched. Second, men as well as cattle are afflicted, but not unto death. Third, men and cattle perish, but are forewarned to escape the hail, which falls irretrievably upon the crops. The element of unity in all these is this, that it is now the industrial activity of the nation that is plagued – not any longer nature energy, but human energy in all its manifold outgoing – the rearing of herbs. The raising of crops, and particularly in that which serves as the central characteristic of the Egyptians' activity, the huge architectural enterprises.

## The Eighth Plague: Locusts

Go unto Pharaoh and caution him. I have hardened his heart strong; stubborn. This does not mean that God on purpose made Pharaoh sinful. For God to make it impossible for a man to obey Him, and then punish him for his disobedience, would be both unjust and contrary to the fundamental belief in freedom of the will. The phrase most often translated "hardening of the heart" occurs nineteen times; ten times it is said that Pharaoh hardened his heart; and nine times the hardening of Pharaoh's heart is ascribed to God. There seems to be two sides to this hardening. When the divine command came to Pharaoh, set the slaves free, and his reply was I will not, each repetition of Pharaoh's persistence obstinacy made it less likely that he would eventually listen to the word of God. For such is the Law of Conscience; every-time the voice of conscience is disobeyed, it becomes duller and feebler and the heart grows harder. Man cannot remain neutral in the presence of duty or of any direct command of God. He either obeys the divine command and it becomes unto him a blessing; or, he defies God and such command then becomes unto him a curse. It is part of the divinely ordered scheme of things that if a man deliberately chooses evil, it proceeds to enslave him; it blinds and stupefies him, making for him repentance well-nigh impossible. Every successive refusal on the part of Pharaoh to listen to the message of Moses froze up his better nature more and more, until it seemed as if God had hardened his heart. But this was only so because Pharaoh had first hardened it himself, and continued doing so. The Omniscient God knew beforehand whether His obstinacy would lead Pharaoh, and prepared Moses for initial failure by warning him that Pharaoh's heart would become hardened. Pharaoh refused to humble himself. This was not the real cause of Pharaoh's sin after all these plagues – refusal to humble himself before God was. And Pharaoh would not really humble himself until he made God's will his own, and fulfilled his oft-given promise to permit the Israelites to leave Egypt. His heart was hardened, but his will was still free, and he could repent if he chose.

> "Else, if thou refuse to let my people go, behold, to-morrow will I bring Locusts into thy border; and they shall cover the face of the earth, that one shall not be able to see the earth; and they shall eat the residue of that is escaped, which remaineth unto you from the hail, and shall eat every tree which growth for you out of the field." (Exodus 10:4,5)

To-morrow – again another opportunity is given to the King to submit himself to the divine command.

They shall cover the face of the earth – these swarm of locusts is a strange sight, beautiful if you can forget the destruction it brings with it. The whole air, to twelve or even eighteen feet above the ground, is filled with the insects, reddish-brown in body, with bright, gauzy wings. When the sun's rays catch them, it is like the seas sparkling with light. When you see them against a cloud, they are like the dense flakes of a driving snowstorm. They blot out the sun above, and cover the ground beneath, and fill the air whichever way one looks. The breeze carries them swiftly past, but they come on in clouds, a host of which there is no end, each of them a harmless creature which you can catch and crush in your hand, but appalling in their power of collective devastation. Their voracity is incredible; (Joel 2:20) not only the leaves, but the branches and even the wood are attached and devoured. The residue here refers to the wheat and the spelt (Exodus 9:32), which escaped the havoc wrought by the hail. If part of a swarm alights on a house, the locusts enter its innermost recesses and fill every corner.

The eighth and ninth plagues are less perceptible: the seventh plague, the hail, seeming to belong both to this group and to the former. It belongs to the former class because like them, it falls on the products of the nation's toil and activity; it belongs to this class because like the darkness, it may be said to be atmospheric. And the points of connection between the eighth plague, the locusts, and the ninth, the darkness, are these: the locusts are derived from lands outside the boundaries of Egypt; and the darkness, which is no doubt to be identified with the hot sirocco wind, of which travelers speak as so terrible, comes also from the hot desert bounding the southern frontiers of the country.

## The Ninth Plague: Darkness

Like the third and sixth plagues, it is inflicted unannounced; and parleying, the driving of a bargain and then breaking it, by which the eighth was attend, is quite enough to account for this. This plague would especially affect the spirits of the Egyptians, whose chief object of worship was ra, the sun-god.

<u>Darkness which may be felt</u> – explained as an aggravation of the wind of the desert, which is not uncommon in Egypt, and is accompanied by weird darkness, beyond that of our worst fogs.

## The Warning of the Tenth Plague: The First <br> Born in the Land of Egypt Shall Die

Moses learns that the last plague would be followed by an immediate departure; and this gave him time to devise measures of preparing the Israelites for the journey. It is affirmed by <u>Jehovah</u>, Himself, that the two-fold object sought to be gained by all the plagues is most conclusively reached in this:

(1)  I will execute judgment on all the gods of Egypt (Exodus 12:12); and
(2)  Ye shall know how that Jehovah doth put a difference between the Egyptians and the Israelites (Exodus 11:7).

The last purpose had been exhibited all along from the third plague; but when the destroyer with fatal precision passed by the homes of Israel, and entered the houses of the Egyptians scattered up and down by their side, filling them with death and lamentation, the difference had never been so fearfully marked before. At the same time, the fact that the angel needed some sign by which to distinguish the houses of Israel from those of Egypt – all being in His sight equally sinful and amenable to judgment; and the kind of sign used, the sprinkled blood of atonement taught the Israelites that it was God's mercy and grace alone that favored them above the people of Egypt with record to the first purpose – execution of judgment on the gods of Egypt. It is less easy to see whether the judgment was direct or immediate, whether the gods themselves died or whether they were shown to be weak and powerless by the death of those whom they should have animated and saved. Perhaps the judgment was of both kinds. The first born of men and cattle fell, from the first born of Pharaoh upon the throne to the first born of the maidservant behind the mill, and all the first born of beasts (Exodus 11:5). The Egyptians paid divine honors to various animals; and the first born of all these beasts were to be doomed.

## A Summary of the Ten Plagues

Pharaoh is the incarnation of sullen force, yielding by inches, or for a single moment, only to harden his heart when the crisis is past. But it is human strength matching itself against the inexhaustible resources of nature, which Moses is permitted to wield.

The river, which is Egypt's pride, runs with blood from out its reed-grass, frogs invade the secret recesses of luxury; the dust of the ground takes life, to become loathsome vermin; indoors and outside, there is no escape from swarming flies and corruption. While all over the land of Egypt beasts are dying of murrain, in Israel's land of Goshen, the cattle are intact. The royal magicians, seeking to compete with the wonders of Moses, become themselves victims to the plague of boils. Now the heaven begins to play their part and rain down wasting hail; while, to enhance the wonder, fire winds about the hailstones and melts them not. The land of Egypt is one mass of desolation; but from outside, the east wind blows steadily until the swarming locusts hide the ground; at a sign from the champion of Israel the western hurricane succeeds, and the locust hosts are swept into the Red Sea. Then the whole scene dissolves into darkness that might be felt; every man a solitary prisoner where he stands. At last, midnight reveals the slain first born and Pharaoh and his people thrust Israel forth.

# CHAPTER VIII
# THE JUDGMENT ON
# JACOB AND ESAU

In this story, I see judgment of self-value. It begins with a birthright. Esau was gifted in hunting. Esau was the rough, outdoor type who roamed the fields skillful in hunting. Jacob was the home-loving type who stayed with his mother in tents. (Genesis 25:27) At a time when Esau came home from a hunting trip, tired and hungry, Jacob saw an opportunity to take the birthright away from him.

(Birthright, Firstborners) In the Law of Moses, it was stipulated that the firstborn should receive a double portion of the inheritance (Deuteronomy 21:17). The firstborn also became head of the patriarchal family and possessed representative privileges. He had the right of dominion over his younger brothers. His authority was extensive and he exercised priestly prerogatives. The birthright also included a spiritual heritage in the promise of God to His chosen people. The blessing was a most important part of the birthright. This constituted something more than the pious wish of a fond parent. It possessed the element of prophecy. God used such a practice to reveal His purpose regarding the one blessed.

Esau sold his birthright to Jacob. After coming in from hunting exhausted and hungry, Esau demanded his brother's pottage, which Jacob had just prepared. But Jacob did not give it to him until Esau had given him the birthright. Esau, rough and crude, could not care less about the birthright as long as he had something to eat (Genesis 25:29-34). Esau's judgment, was it based on fleshly value or spiritual value? He chose the fleshly value. He cared less about God because he spent less time with God, but spent more time with worldly things. By misjudging his value, Esau lost his first place blessing and came in second to his youngest brother. Because of that, Jacob inherited the divine promise made to Abraham (Genesis 12:3). The dew of heaven – in those countries where the days are hot and the nights are cold, the dew is very abundant and drenches the ground. It is essential to vegetation during the rainless summer and was therefore regarded as a divine blessing. When Esau lost his first place blessing, he wept, just plain out crying because of his judgment of value. Those tears of Esau, the sensuous wild impulsive man, almost like the cry of some "trapped" creature. Now he has to serve his younger brother. But Jacob will have to pay for his judgment of pretending to be Esau and robbed him out of his blessing. Esau saw his brother Jacob as a supplanted (outwitted). Let me tell you a Bible story:

'Now Laban had two daughters; the name of the elder was Leah, and the younger was Rachel, and Leah's eyes were weak; but Rachel was of beautiful form and fair to look upon. And Jacob loved Rachel; and he said, *"I will serve thee seven years for Rachel thy younger daughter?* And Laban said, *"It is better that I give her to thee, than that I should give her to another man; abide with me.* And Jacob served seven years for Rachel; and they seemed unto him but a few days, for the love he had to her. And Jacob said unto Laban, "Give my my wife for my days are fulfilled, that I may go in unto her." And Laban gathered together all the men of the place, and made a feast. And it came to pass in the evening that he took Leah his daughter, and brought her to him; and he went in unto her. And Laban gave Zilphah his handmaid unto his daughter Leah for a handmaid. And it came to pass in the morning that behold, it was Leah; and he said to Laban, *"What is this thou hast done unto me? Did not I serve with thee for Rachel? Wherefore then hast thou <u>beguiled</u> me?"* (Genesis 29:16-25)

Now, let me tell you another Bible story:

"Be not deceived; God is not mocked: For whatsoever a man soweth, <u>that</u> shall he also reap." (Galatians 6:7)"

Notice that I underlined the word that. Whatever that is, will come back to you, as a farmer sows seeds into the ground and reap his harvest. It is a saying that you reap what you sow. Jacob sowed <u>beguild</u> (outwit), now he is reaping <u>beguild</u>. Because of that, Jacob had to work fourteen years for Rachel, the woman he loved. Because he judged to outwit his brother Esau, also at a young age he had to leave home from his mother and his dying father. Two brothers are born with two different judgments.

# CHAPTER IX
# THE LAST JUDGMENT OF EPHRAIM

When Rehoboam ascended the throne of his father, Solomon, it was Jeroboam I, an Ephramite, who led the Northern tribes to rebel and form their own nation (I Kings 12:12-20). Yet, this was ordained of God in punishment for Judah's and Israel's sins (I Kings 11:26-40). The prophets made it clear that the sins of the rulers and people of Ephraim brought upon them God's judgment (Isaiah 28:1; Hosea 10:9-15).

Jehu was the instrument of God to execute His judgment upon the house of Ahab. But he came to the throne through dastardly crimes of blood-guiltiness (II Kings 9:14 and following). True, his act was commended (II Kings 10:30), for it was such in itself, but later events showed the motivating causes in Jehu's life had been pride and ambition. The prophet Hosea's pronouncement had point here, for Jeroboam II then reigning was of Jehu's house. God would not only visit that house because it had gone into idolatry, but all Israel with the destruction of their kingdom because of their gross departure from the Lord.

It is clear from the Prophet Habakkuk that Israel was ripe for judgment because of evil on every hand. God requires truth in the inward parts, and He wants such in the hearts of others as well as Israel. The hour for Israel, the Northern Kingdom, has struck and her punishments is inevitable. She is ripe for the judgment and it draws on apace. But God promises at the same time that His wrath will not go forth against Judah at the same hour. For them He had reserved mercy, yet deliverance, to be brought about by no human agency, but solely by the power of God.

The defeat of Sennacherib before Jerusalem at the end of the eighth century B.C., when 185,000 were slain by the angel of Jehovah in one night

(II Kings 19 and Isaiah 37), was a glorious fulfillment of this prediction, but the prophecies of all the prophets are luminous with promises of the future (tribulation), complete deliverance (physical) and salvation (spiritual) of Israel. Notice the three marks of time: "many days", "afterward", and "in the latter days", which are of vital importance here as elsewhere in prophetic scriptures. Here are the three elements in Israel's future: return, seek, and come with fear. The whole nation of Israel is in view with particular emphasis on the Northern Kingdom of Israel. Notice how repeatedly Ephraim appears at the head of these chapters of Hosea (chp. 4:1) to the end of the book.

Ephraim is so bound up with idols that he will not be severed from them. The Northern Kingdom is held by idolatry as though under a spell, bewitched by it and utterly helpless in himself to extricate himself. He has so wholly given himself, to his senseless idols, that only judgment remains. The judgment of God is toward all. Such continuance in ill-doing can only issue in the devastating judgment of God. Hosea, speaks about "The Trumpet to Thy Mouth", "As An Eagle Against the House of Jehovah!" (It seems to view the tribulation.) The watchman is to put the trumpet to his mouth to warn the people of the oncoming invasion (twenty-one judgments in the tribulation). Ephraim is charged with five accounts that causes for the coming judgment here predicted (Hosea 8:1-11):

(1) Transgression of the covenant and trespass against God's Law;
(2) Setting up Kings and princes without God's direction;
(3) Idolatry;
(4) The sin of seeking help from Assyria; and
(5) Idolatrous and sinful altars.

What the scourging east wind does to fruit, the Assyrian, the chastening rod of the Lord, will perform upon Ephraim in spite of his fruitfulness. The hot and parching wind will dry up the springs and fountains, and the enemy will take all the nation's treasures as spoil. The transgressor who finds no delight in the revealed ways of the Lord, will find the purpose of God and will condemn him in the hour of judgment (Tribulation).

When Ephraim spoke (Hosea 8:1) a rapid resume of the history of the Northern Kingdom coming to an end - At first Ephraim's power was great, and he was feared by surrounding tribes. Jeroboam, the first King of the ten tribes, was an Ephraimite. He sinned and led Israel to sin, through the calf-worship which he had set up at Dan and Beersheba.

Baal – (I Kings 16:31)i

Died – spiritually; yet literally too, for Baal-worship was a cause of the national decay and final downfall.

<u>Morning cloud</u> – is a figure of speech to represent the swift and complete extinction of the Northern Kingdom. The morning cloud which passes as one observes it, the chaff scattered by the whirlwind, the smoke of the chimney – all leave no trace behind; so shall it be with the Kingdom Israel.

# CHAPTER X
# THE JUDGMENT OF JONAH

The judgment on Jonah was because of his disobedience to the call of God. God's word to Jonah was a clear and unmistakable command to go to heathen Nineveh and preach against it because of its grievous wickedness. God commanded Jonah to go, but he was of a contrary mind. He fled to Tarshish. Because of Jonah's disobedience to God, He (God) brought a tremendous wind upon the sea. There was such a violent storm at sea that it seemed the ship would break up. The storm only blew around Jonah's ship, whereas others sailed by on perfectly calm waters (Jonah 1:7). The wind came from all four directions, as in Job 1:19. Jonah's disobedience caused trouble for the men that were on the ship. The men said to Jonah, "Why is this terrible thing happening to us?" Jonah answered saying, "I fear God, the Lord of the heaven, who made the sea and the dry land." The men (sailors) retorted, "If you are really so righteous, then why did God bring this storm upon us?" They then hoisted Jonah and threw him overboard, and the sea's raging ceased. God had a special fish that he had prepared (I believe sometime during creation), a large fish just at this appointed time for Jonah. God then summoned this large fish, which He had prepared to swallow Jonah, by the time Jonah hit the water, the large fish was already there. Jonah remained inside the fish's belly for three days and three nights, because of his disobedience to God's call, and doing or not going on the greatest mission to Nineveh. God rescued Jonah because He was not finished with him. The fish was large enough to swallow Jonah whole without injuring his body; Jonah survived even though he had no oxygen to breathe. God joined him to the fish in the same way an embryo is joined to its mother through the umbilical cord. Despite the anguish he experienced, he succeeded in maintaining his sanity and calm to such a degree that he was able to compose a thanksgiving prayer to God. Because of his suffering inside the fish's belly, Jonah said, "In my misery I called out to God, and God answered him." Jonah cried out from the belly of sheol, you cast me into deep waters, into mighty seas, and the river engulfed me. All your breakers and waves swept over me. I thought I was driven from your sight. The waters surrounded me so that I almost died. I sank to the bottom of the (underwater) mountains; the earth closed its bolts on me forever. But you, God, my Lord, lifted my life up from the pit." From this I would think that Jonah stayed in the water for quite some time before the fish swallowed him. God kept him alive through such terrible sufferings in order that his sins (of disobedience) be atoned for. Jonah thought that he would never return to the land, or he will die. As I said before, I believe that the fish that swallowed Jonah was created for this purpose during the six days of creation.

Jonah was able to stand inside the fish, and light reached to him through its two eyes, which were like glass windows. Although Jonah's head was inside the fish, he speaks of the fish's head as if it were his own. Jonah refers to his own head, describing what he experienced after the male (dag) fish disgorged him into the water, but before the female (dagga) fish arrived to swallow him up. (I don't mean to confuse you with words!)

After all of this, Jonah finally surrendered to God, "When my soul became faint, I remembered God." So Jonah was spared. God directed the fish and the fish spewed Jonah onto dry land. Jonah's wrong judgment on himself of disobedience caused him all of this, when he didn't have to.

# CHAPTER XI
# THE JUDGMENT SEAT OF CHRIST

The Judgment Seat of Christ will follow the rapture of the Church.

> "For we (the saints) must all appear before the Judgment Seat of Christ; that every one may receive the things done in his body, according to that he hath done, whether it is good or bad." (Romans 14:10)

An abiding conviction that each individual will stand at the Judgment Seat of Christ, and receive according to the deeds done in the body, is adapted to make men circumspect, and lead them most earnestly to desire and diligently to labor that they may be accepted of Him. At the Judgment Seat of Christ, there will be the assignment of rewards. Rewards must be earned by faithful living and serving. (I Corinthians 9:25; II Timothy 4:8; James 1:12; II John 8) Every person who ever lives must keep an appointment with Christ at the final judgment. Believers will be rewarded, unbelievers will be punished eternally. The freedom God has given to us comes with the price tag of responsibility. As Sovereign Lord and creator of the world and all its people, God is also the Judge before whom we all must stand. Every person must give an account to God. In a sense, judgment comes daily as God interacts with our lives. But we also face a final judgment in the end time. This judgment poses no threat to the Christian, so far as our eternal destiny is concerned. We have already been pronounced forgiven through the saving work of Jesus Christ, and caught-up in the rapture. Each of us may still expect to give an account to God for what we have done with our lives. The Apostle Paul states:

"By the grace God has given me, I laid a foundation as an expert builder, and someone else is building on it. But each one should be careful how he builds. For no one can lay any foundation other than the one already laid, which is Jesus Christ. If any man builds on this foundation using gold, silver, costly stones, wood, hay or straw, his work will be shown for what it is, because the day will bring it to light. It will be revealed with fire, and fire will test the quality of each man's work. If what he has built survives, he will receive his reward. If it is burned up, he will suffer loss; he himself will be saved, but only as one escaping through the flames (I Corinthians 3:10-15).

Apostle Paul exhorts the Corinthians to be careful in choosing the builders and materials to be used. For in due time, every man's work is shown. That is, wrong teaching would be exposed and teachers are rewarded accordingly. Jesus is the foundation; the Church is the Holy Temple of God. Anyone who destroys this Temple will be destroyed. The glory of this living temple belongs to God and not to any builders who receive a reward for their work. Thinking I am innocent does not make me so. God is the only Judge. We should not worry about how people judge us, nor should we appoint ourselves Judge over others. We should seek to be ready for the day of His judgment. Christ is the final Judge who will reveal human motives. He has not called us to be judge of any other person. Accurate judgment requires the ability to know and take into account that which has been done in secret from human eyes. It requires that motives behind the outward acts be taken into consideration. The positive aspect of final judgment is that praise will be given the worthy just as condemnation will be given the unworthy. The warning is clear that motives for service and ministry will be clear to God and a major factor in His judgment. The believers are in some way to participate in judging the world. Because of spiritual union with Christ, to whom God has committed all judgment, believers share His work with Him (John 5:21-24).

Also, there is to be participation in judging angels. Most likely the reference is to disobedient angels, such as are mentioned in Jude 6. This judgment of the believers is the works which is acceptable and that which is worthless. Let's go back to our high school graduation; how that some were honored for what they had achieved, and those who didn't. But they all walked across the stage. It will be a shame living all those years and have not achieved what God expects out of us. That, which determines whether one receives, or loses a reward, is the trial by fire (II Corinthians 5:10). The gold, silver, and costly stones are indestructible materials. These are the work of God, which man only appropriates and uses. The wood, hay and stubble are destructible materials. These are the work of men which man has produced by his own effort. The Apostle Paul is revealing the fact that the examination at the Seat of Christ is to determine that which was done by God through the individual and that which the individual did in his own strength; that which was done for the glory of God and that which was done for the glory of the flesh. It cannot be determined by outward observation into which class any <u>work</u> falls, so that work must be put into the crucible in order that its true character may be proved. In this test, there will be two decisions. There will be lost of reward for that which is proven by the fire to be destructible. Things done in the strength and for the glory of the flesh, regardless of what the act might be, will be disapproved (I Corinthians 9:27). The awarding of the prize for successful running following strict training indicates the judgment in view has to do with service and rewards; rewards are earned. The symbolism of reward for Christians is the victor's crown. It is possible to be disqualified from receiving rewards. Failure to remain disciplined and faithful courts a disqualification. St. John states:

"Watch out that you do not lose what you have worked for, but that you may be rewarded fully." (II John 8).

John issued an earnest plea that Christians guard themselves against sin and the consequent loss of rewards. The fact that rewards worked for can be lost, promotes the faithlessness. Continuance in the faith and in obedience to Christ's commands gain a full reward. There will be a reward bestowed for that work that is proved to be indestructible by the fire test. In the New Testament there are five areas in which specific mention is made of a reward:

(1) An incorruptible crown for those who set mastery over the old man. (I Corinthians 9;25)
(2) A crown of rejoicing for the soul winners (I Thessalonians 2:19). Saved people are the fruit and reward of faithful evangelism. Seeing people saved is the joy and glory of those who faithfully witness.
(3) A crown of life for those enduring trials (James 1:12) and bears his trials with a right spirit. Judgment does not always mean punishment. God is the just Judge who will reward the faithful.
(4) A crown of righteousness for loving His appearing (II Timothy 4:8). Christ's final judgment will include rewards for all who have centered life on Him and His promises.
(5) A crown of glory for being willing to feed the flock of God (I Peter 5:4). The Chief Shepherd is Jesus Christ who, at His coming will reward all those who minister faithfully to His flocks. Pastors of God are likened to Shepherds of sheep and are encouraged to be faithful. Those who do will receive their reward when the Chief Shepherd appears.

The Apostle Paul chooses to describe the rewards as being associated with honor and dignity bestowed on the over-comer. The greater the reward, greater is the bestowed capacity to bring glory to God. Right after the Judgment Seat has been taken, then the "Marriage of the Lamb." The marriage itself must be placed between the Judgment Seat of Christ and the Second Coming of Christ. The Marriage of the Lamb is an event which involves only Christ and the Church. The figure of marriage is used in both the New and Old Testaments to describe God's relation to His people (Hosea 2:19-21; Ephesians 5:25-27). The consummation of the Church as the Bride of Christ will involve the completion of individual salvation and resultant corporate righteousness of the body, the Church. Eternal union with Christ is the Church's destiny and hope. The marital relationship is sharply focused to describe the Church. The Bride makes herself ready for the coming of the <u>Lamb</u> for the marriage. The Church prepares for the wedding by witness, by right living, and by those actions which please the Lamb. The Church must remain morally pure as it waits for the Bridegroom's (Jesus Christ) appearance. St John states in Revelation 19:7:

> "Let us be glad and rejoice, and give honour to Him; for the marriage
> of the Lamb is come and His wife hath mad herself ready."

The term "Lamb" means Christ, that is, the Lamb of God. This name was given to Jesus by John. "The next day John seeth Jesus coming unto him, and saith, 'Behold the Lamb of God, which taketh away the sin of the world.' (John 1:29)." The wife of the Lamb is the Church of Christ, which He has purchased with His blood (Acts 20:28). The Church is likened to a bride. Hosea spoke of Israel as an unfaithful and estranged wife because she had gone after other gods. She had been rejected and then restored:

> "And I will betroth thee unto me forever; yea, I will betroth thee unto
> me in righteousness, and in judgment; and in loving kindness, and
> in mercies." (Hosea 2:19)

The marriage of the Lamb and His wife is symbolic of union of Christ with the true Church. The garments of fine linen denote chastity and purity. Before this marriage will take place, the Church must purge itself of evil and become righteous and worthy to be called the wife of Christ, who purchased her with His blood. The whiteness of linen represents holiness (Revelation 19:7). During the Tribulation, the saints were in heaven preparing for this important event. The Marriage of the Lamb is a heavenly scene; therefore, the Bride, the Lamb's wife, could hardly be Israel, because the Israelites are promised one more week to make up the seventh week and that is the Tribulation.

I believe the Bride of Christ is that Church whom Christ gave Himself, and which will be presented to Him "holy and without blemish", is made up of those saints from Pentecost to the rapture (Ephesians 5:25-27). This is the full and final union between Christ and His Church.

# CHAPTER XII
# THE JUDGMENTS OF
# THE TRIBULATION

This entire tribulation period is a period characterized by judgments from the hand of the Lord. It is the Lord's Day.

I.   <u>The Seals</u>. The opening of the sealed scroll by the Son of God is given in the Book of Revelation, Chapter 6. Here is the beginning of the unfolding of the Judgment of God. They are mainly divine judgments through human agencies. They fall upon the earth in the first portion of the tribulation and they will continue on through the period.

II.   <u>The meaning of the symbols of the horses of the seals</u>.

(1)   <u>The White Horse.</u> – White is symbolical of purity and power. The bow indicated conquest and expansion of the realm. This vision of horses is similar to the vision of chariots with horses of different colors, which was seen by the Prophet Zechariah (Zecharia 1:8; 6:1-7). The horses denote dispensations, the character of which is indicated by their color and the other emblems employed. A white horse is the symbol of victory.
<u>The First Seal</u> – represents the peace movement on the earth. It may be associated with the covenant made by the Beast to establish peace on earth, then later break it.

(2)   <u>The Red Horse.</u> – Reddish brown,; they are noted for their speed and endurance. Red is the symbol of blood and the red horse symbolizes

great destruction of life (Nahum 2:3). Red; an emblem of war and bloodshed.

The Second Seal – represents the removal of peace from the earth and the wars that engulf the earth.

(3) The Black Horse. Black; a symbol of devastation, mourning and woe.
Balances; indicating that food would be but scantily supplied.
A Measure; about enough to sustain a man for a day.
A Penny; the price of a day's labor. The oil and the wine; these would be needed to keep men from starving, so great would be the scarcity of food (Revelation 6:5,6). A black horse is also symbolical of death, famine and destruction. Black, like darkness, is the symbol of mourning and despair. The balances (scales) are symbolical of justice. Death, famine and destruction were at hand, the people had gone astray, corruption and injustice prevailed. The old order was ready to be destroyed and a new order, based on justice, was to be substituted. This new order could not come without suffering. Whenever evil is removed, the good usually suffer with the bad. Famine, death and destruction are followed by a period of prosperity or vise-versa. This is generally the case. (Genesis 41:18-28) A measure of wheat for a penny indicates that food must be abundant because of a period of prosperity.
The Third Seal – represents famine that results from the desolation of war.

(4) The Pale Horse. The Pale Horse represents death, famine and destruction. Death is the wages of sin and disobedience, which often accompany a period of luxury and prosperity. Injustice, greed and lawlessness cause men and animals to suffer alike.
A pale horse; the original denotes the ghastly paleness of a corpse.
Hell; that is, Hades, the abode of the dead. Hades follows death to swallow in its abyss those whom death has slain.
The Fourth Seal – prefigures the death that follows in the wake of the failure of men to establish peace.

The First Seal was opened revealing a man on a white horse, who had a bow, who went forth to conquer. The Lord Jesus shall come on a white horse, but this is not He, but a fake Christ, who establishes a temporary peace. Listening to the first prediction of Matthew; twenty-four, "Many shall come in my name, saying I am Christ (vs. 5).

Let's compare the two riders on the white horses:

53

In Revelation 6:2 is the beginning of the tribulation period. This rider comes with a bow, but without an arrow, indicating that he offers a promise of peace.

> "And I saw, and behold a white horse; and he that sat on him had a bow; and a crown was given unto him; and he went forth conquering, and to conquer." (Revelation 6:2)

In Revelation 19:2, is at the end of the tribulation period. The rider on the white horse in the First Seal, I believe to be the Anti-Christ, he has a <u>bow</u> and a <u>crown</u> (στέφανος - stephanos). But the rider in Revelation 19:12, wore a crown (διαδήματα – diadema), and Christ's weapon is a sword. He comes imitating Christ and offering peace, but he is as false as is the peace he offers.

> "And I saw heaven opened, and behold a white horse; and he that sat upon him was called faithful and true, and righteousness he doth judge and make war." (Revelation 19:2)

Here is the beginning of the tribulation, which starts with the First Seal. Judgment is about to fall. All the acts described under the seven seals are acts of judgment. As each seal is opened, God's judicial action is disclosed, one stage at a time. The Apostle John could hear the sound like as of thunder coming from heaven, the thundering voice speaks of coming judgment. This thundering sounds the beginning of the tribulation period. The thunder of divine judgment upon the earth rolls with increasing crescendo for seven years until the lightening of Christ's Second Coming to the earth strikes. (Matthew 24:27; Revelation 19:11)

<u>The Second Seal</u> sent forth a red horse and its rider. The red horse represents a bloody warfare. The effort to bring universal peace that is not of Christ will fail, and this failure will result in strife, violence, and bloodshed. The devil (great red dragon) was a murderer from the beginning. (John 8:44; Revelation 12:3) The rider on the red horse has a sword. He proceeds to take peace from the earth and to kill. At first, the Anti-Christ seems to be a man of peace, but when they shall say peace and safety; then sudden destruction cometh upon them (I Thessalonians 5:3). Red is the appropriate color of communism, and all the world knows what a bloodthirsty lot the reds are: Russia, China, North Korea and Czechoslovakia. <u>Watch the future</u>.

Jesus said,

"And ye shall hear of wars and rumors of wars . . . for nation shall rise against nation, ad kingdom against kingdom." (Matthew 24:6-7)

They shall kill one another;

"Every man's sword shall be against his brother (Ezekiel 38:21)

The rider upon the red horse is most likely the same that rode the white horse, but now reveals his identity. He is not the prince of peace, but satan's counterfeit, an impostor.

The Third Seal is the same rider upon a black horse. This time he holds no weapon of warfare in his hands, but a pair of scales. These balances, like the black horse, suggest scarcity to the extent of famine. Food rationing of the strictest order is an aftermath of war. Black follows red; famine follows war. Famine is symbolized in scripture by the color black. "Our skin was black like an oven because of the terrible famine." (Lamentations 5:10)

When our Lord Jesus said that there shall be wars and rumors of wars with nation rising against nation, and kingdom against kingdom, He added, "And there shall be famines." (Matthew 24:7) The famine during the tribulation suggested "a measure of wheat for a penny, and three measures of barley for a penny." Here the word measure means the amount required to feed a man for one day. A man has to work one full day to stay alive, also to divide that food with his family. This was happening while the war was going on. The rider with the balances speaks of food conservation. That black day is coming to all who miss the rapture. The day of famine will appear upon the earth. This is why this period is called the tribulation.

The Fourth Seal comes on a pale horse and the rider is called death, the aftermath of war and famine. There have been furious wars, famines and death-dealing plagues in the past, but nothing comparable to this event which is still future. Its fury is depicted in its widespread effects, killing one fourth of the earth population. This is the result of the foregoing judgments which God call, "My Four Sore Judgments" (Ezekiel 14:21).

The fourth rider is named Death, the final claimant and custodian of the body. Hell followed after him to gather the souls of the victims. Hell, the abode of the un-generated souls that leave the body at death is an ally of death. Hell or Hades is the abode of departed spirits between death and resurrection. It is temporary in contrast to the Lake of Fire which is forever (Revelation 20:13-14). After all unredeemed men have heard the final word of judgment, death and hell (everyone in hell will go with hell), were cast into the Lake of Fire (Revelation 20:14). Don't you be there to see the horror of the coming tribulation.

The Fifth Seal reveals clearly that some on earth will turn to God after the Church has been raptured. There will be those saved during the tribulation, but they will pay with their lives. (Why? When you can accept Jesus Christ and live a righteous life, then be raptured with the Church.) Following the prophecy of Jesus Christ in Matthew 24:5-7, Jesus added, "Then shall they deliver you up to be afflicted, and they shall kill you; and ye shall be hated of all nations for my name's sake." (Matthew 24:9) These are the martyrs of the tribulation days. Having heard the gospel of the kingdom, thousands will believe and receive it, but they will be persecuted by the Beast.

The tribulation saints will be living in the dispensation of judgment. Their cry for vengeance explains somewhat the imprecatory Psalms, "The cry, How long?", (I got to get out of here.) is the familiar Jewish cry during the time of Jacob's trouble (Psalm 74:9-10; 79:5; 89:46; and 94:3-4). It is the time of judgment, the Judgment Throne is set. They are crying but they are told to wait patiently (while they are suffering), until more of their brethren and fellow-servants are slain for their faith. In Revelation, chapter thirteen, it describes how severe will be the persecution of Jews by the Anti-Christ. There can be no response to their cry until the martyred band is complete.

The Sixth Seal results in catastrophe on a world-wide scale. This is not the final judgment; it is not the end of the world. There are three great earthquakes mentioned in Revelation 6:12; 11:13; and 16:18-19. This is the first of the three. The judgments issuing from the first four seals were at the hands of the Anti-Christ, but with the opening of the sixth seal, the judgments are supernatural and come from heaven. Earthquakes have occurred in the past when God acted in judgment. Mount Sinai quaked when God descended upon it in the fire (Exodus 20:18-19), and the people recognized the quake for what it was (Exodus 20:18-19). In the days of Elijah there was an earthquake which broke rocks in pieces (I Kings 19:11). When Jesus Christ died on the cross of Calvary, there was an earthquake (Matthew 27:51-52).

This sixth seal judgment was foretold by our Lord Jesus Christ when He said, "And there shall be signs in the sun, and in the moon, and in the stars; and upon the earth distress of nations, with perplexity; the sea and the waves roaring; men's hearts failing them for fear and for looking after those things which are coming on the earth. For the powers of heaven shall be shaken."

(Luke 21:25-26) The people who will be living on the earth at that time will actually see the fulfillment of the astronomical signs in connection with the heavenly bodies.

Jesus Christ then added the time element of these happenings, "And then shall ye see the Son of man coming in a cloud with power and great glory." (Luke 21:27) Receive Jesus Christ while there is yet time, for the day of His judgment must surely come. Before the seventh seal, in the midst of wrath, God remembers mercy (Habakkuk 3:2), and suspends judgment. The judgment winds have been blowing, but now there is a lull in the storm. God stops the storm in order to show mercy to those who will accept it. The instruments God uses in suspending judgment are His servants, the angels.

The Great Tribulation is about to break upon the earth with the opening of The Seventh Seal, but the fifth angel ascending from the east, restrains the four from proceeding, and judgment is suspended. The judgments which issue forth from the first six seals are only "the beginning of sorrows" (Matthew 24:8; Mark 13:8). The Great Tribulation referred to by the Lord Jesus Christ (Matthew 24:21), and by Daniel, the Prophet (Daniel 9:27; 11:31; and 12:11), begins with the sounding of the trumpets, which sounding issues forth from the seventh seal.

The Great Tribulation is held back <u>till</u> the sealing of the Jews (Revelation 7:4-8).

"And I heard the number of them which were sealed: and there were sealed an hundred and forty and four thousand of all the tribes of the children of Israel. Of the tribes of Judah, were sealed twelve thousand of the tribes of Reuben were sealed twelve thousand of the tribes of Gad were sealed twelve thousand of the tribes of Aser were sealed twelve thousand. Of the tribes of Mannasses were sealed twelve thousand. Of the tribes of Simeon were sealed twelve thousand. Of the tribes of Levi were sealed twelve thousand. Of the tribes of Issachar were sealed twelve thousand. Of the tribes of Zabulon were sealed twelve thousand. Of the tribes of Joseph were sealed twelve thousand. Of the tribes of Benjamin were sealed twelve thousand." (Revelation 7:4-8)

Judgment is suspended till 144,000 Jews were sealed.

With the opening of The Seventh Seal, we are introduced to the sounding of the seven trumpets. The seventh seal includes the seven trumpets.

"And when He had opened the seventh seal, there was silence in heaven about the space of half and hour." (Revelation 8:1)

Here there is a stillness and a silence, no voice is heard; no motion is seen. But the next time His voice is heard throughout all the earth, judgment will fall upon the unbelieving world of men.

III. <u>The Seven Trumpets</u>

The seven angels in Revelation, chapter 8, verse 2; hold the prerogative to announce the execution of judgment through the sounding of the trumpets. But, they are restrained for a space of about half an hour. These are solemn moments because of the judgment which is to follow. This is the silent, solemn preparation for the most awful judgments ever to come upon the world. They are the judgments prophesied by Enoch (Jude 14).

The seven seals suggest the seven secrets which are to be revealed. The seven trumpets signify that the secrets will be disclosed and published. In warning his hearers not to publish their deeds of charity, Jesus said, "When thou doest thine alms, do not sound a trumpet before thee (Matthew 6:2).

In this case, each trumpet is to announce a woe. The Great Tribulation will be sevenfold. Each woe will be announced by an angel. The great catastrophe will be followed by a period of restoration and salvation. Many men will survive and triumph over these tribulations (Revelation 7:14). These and a remnant of Israel will be saved and receive the great reward of eternal life for the suffering, which they endured for the sake of their faith.

(1) <u>Hail and Fire mingled with blood; Hail-Fire-Blood</u>: symbols of slaughter and ruin.

<u>The First Trumpet</u> – presents a judgment that falls upon the earth, in which a third of the inhabitants are slain.

(2) <u>Great mountain burning with fire. The third part-died</u>; and the third part of the ships were destroyed showing that great numbers would perish, businesses suspended and vast amounts of property destroyed.

<u>The Second Trumpet</u> – presents a judgment that falls upon the sea and, again a third part of the inhabitants are slain.

(3) <u>A great star from Heaven</u> – the name of the star is called Wormwood. <u>Wormwood</u>; indicating the bitter and fatal distresses which the presence of this star would produce upon the wicked, especially the persecutors of God's people. Continuance in sin inevitably leads

to misery; and the greatness of the numbers, wealth, and power of persevering transgressors will do nothing towards diminishing the certainty, the greatness, or the perpetuity of their torment.

The Third Trumpet – presents a judgment that falls upon the rivers and fountains of waters. This may depict judgment upon those from whom living water is taken away because they believed the lie (II Thessalonians 2:11).

(4)  The sun, the moon, and the star were smitten.
     The third part of the sun-moon-stars; for the darkening of the heavenly bodies, as the symbol of the overthrow of nations. However, great or long continued the calamities of the wicked in this world, they are only warnings and foretastes of greater and more lasting calamities which if they continue in sin, will suffer in the world to come.

The Fourth Trumpet – is a judgment coming on the sun, moon and stars. This may represent the judgment of God upon world rulers.

(5)  The bottomless pit
     A smoke out of the Bottomless Pit; the smoke arising out of the bottomless pit and darkening the sun and air. Out of this smoke come the swarms of locusts. These fierce invaders had their origin in this satanic delusion, and were thoroughly animated by its spirit. These locusts represent cruel enemies sent by God to scourge those men which have not the seal of God.

Five months; the period of the duration of natural locusts; it here denotes a time appointed and limited by God. They will torment men five months. The description of the Locusts:

". . . the shapes of the locusts were like unto horses prepared unto battle; and on their heads were as it were crowns like gold and their faces were as the faces of men. They had hair as the hair of women, and their teeth were as teeth of Lions. And they had breastplates, as it were breastplates of iron; and the sound of their wings was as the sound of chariots of many horses running to battle. And they had tails like unto scorpions, and there were stings in their tails; and their power was to hurt men five months." (Revelation 9:7-10)

Suppose you are left behind and in the tribulation period? These demonic creatures will come and find you wherever you may be and sting you. Knowing how terrible the pain is, those locusts will come back and back again, time after time for five months and you cannot die because death will run from you. Just imagine after being stung with those unbearable pains, you can hear the sound of those locusts coming back to sting you again; sounding like horses going to battle. When wicked men here suffer a part only of the evils which their sins deserve, life itself often becomes a burden, and they seek for death to relieve them. But there is effectual and permanent relief only in forsaking their sins and turning heartily to the Lord, who will then abundantly pardon. In corrupting and ruining men, the wicked on earth and in hell unite under one great leader; showing that they belong to the same company, are engaged in the same work, and are preparing for the same torment. God's messengers of vengeance: (1) The Seven Seals, (2) The Seven Trumpets, and (3) The Seven Vials; they are often for a season restrained; but when restraints are removed, they commence their work of desolation. No judgments of heaven which men endure will, without the grace of God, lead them to repentance, make them holy or fit them for heaven.

The Fifth Trumpet, which is the first woe, pictures an individual energized by hell, who can let torments of unprecedented dimension loose on the earth. It is generally accepted that these are not literal locusts in that they do not feed on that which is natural to the locust. These are demonic locusts from "hell", the bottomless pit.
The Sixth Trumpet – the four horns of the Golden Altar.
Golden altar-the altar of incense, which stood in the outer sanctuary immediately before the Ark of the Covenant where God dwelt between the Cherubim and, from which it was separated by the inner veil.
Loose the four angels-representing desolating powers which in the course of providence, and being restrained, but were to be suffered for a time to scourge, desolate and destroy a great portion of the earth.

> "And the four angels were loosed, which were prepared for an hour, and a day, and a month, and a year (391 days), for to slay the third part of men. And the number of the army of the horsemen were two hundred thousand, thousand: and I heard the number of them. And thus I saw the horses in the vision, and them that sat on them, having breastplates of fire, and of jacinth, and brimstone: and the heads of the horses were as the heads of lions; and out of their mouths issued fire and smoke and brimstone. By these three was the third part of men killed, by fire, and by smoke, and by the brimstone, which issued out of their mouths. For their power is in their mouth, and in their tails: for their tails were like unto serpents, and had heads, and with them they do hurt (Revelation 9:15-19).

Fire-smoke-brimstone: symbols of their awfully destructive power. The rest of the men; men in the countries, which were overrun by those destroyers who were not killed.

Repented not-this and the preceding judgment had no influence to bring them to repent of their worship of demons and idols. Murders-sorcerers-fornication-thefts; by continuing, to commit these various crimes, they were ripening for still further manifestations of divine wrath.

The sixth trumpet, which is the second woe, is seen to be a great army turned loose to march with destructive force across the face of the earth. The two woes will be great marching armies, one against Israel and one against the Gentiles, which will destroy a third of the earth population.

The Seventh Trumpet.

Great voices in heaven; rejoicing over the rapid and triumphant spread of the Gospel. The time of the dead, that they should be judged; probably meaning the time when the pious dead, who have been slain for Christ's sake, shall be avenged.

Lightening-thundering-earthquakes and great hail; emblems of God's presence, and of the judgments about to be executed on the persecutors of His people.

The seventh trumpet and the third woe judgment bring about the return of Christ to the earth and the subsequent destruction of all hostile powers at the conclusion of the Armageddon program. The middle of the tribulation begins with the rise of great military powers that are aligning themselves. Such would correspond to the first trumpet. Former kingdoms are overthrown, which brings death, as in the second trumpet. A great leader will arise, the Beast, in the third trumpet. His rise will bring about the overthrow of governments and authorities as in the fourth trumpet. There will be great military governments in the period. The armies of the Northern confederacy will invade the land, as in the fifth trumpet and Gentile powers will jockey for position, which causes great destruction, as in the sixth trumpet. These will all be climaxed by the second coming of Christ, as seen in the seventh trumpet.

## The Seven Vials or Bowls

The third series of judgments, which complete the outpouring of divine wrath, are the vials (Revelation 16:1-21). Although four of these vials are poured out on the same areas as the trumpets, they do not seem to be the same judgments. The trumpets being in the middle of the tribulation and depict events during the entire second half of the tribulation. The vials seem to cover a very brief period at the end of the tribulation just prior to the second coming of Christ. These Bowls seem to have particular reference to unbelievers as they undergo the special wrath of God, (Revelation 16:9 and11) and have special reference to the Beast and his followers (Revelation 16:2).

The First Bowl
"And I heard a great voice out of the temple, saying to the seven angels, go your ways, and pour out the vials of the wrath of God upon the earth." (Revelation 1 6:1)

Out of the temple; coming from the temple, where God dwelt. The Holy Scriptures refer all the judgments which fall upon the world for its wickedness to God as their author. They come from him, and execute His Holy purposes. The first vial poured out upon the earth. signifying that some distressing judgment falls on the worshippers of the Beast (all Beast-worshippers).
The Second Vial; poured out upon the sea; a symbol of revolutions accompanied with a terrible amount of bloodshed and preparing the way for the overthrow of the Beast.
The Third Vial; poured out upon the rivers and fountains of waters.
Rivers and Fountains – became blood; seeming to indicate a succession of bloody wars. The result of this judgment is spiritual death. The sea here is seen to become lifeless, as the blood of a dead man.
The Fourth Vial; poured out upon the sun.
Upon the sun; not extinguishing him, but kindling in him an unnatural and scorching heat.

"And men were scorched with great heat, and blasphemed the name of God, which hath power over these plagues: and they repented not to give him glory (Revelations 16:9)

They repented not; they grew no better under their torment, being given up to hardness of heart and blindness of mind. This seems that an individual is envisioned is seen in that the sun is referred to as "him." This may have reference to the judgment of God that imposes blindness upon the Beast's followers.
The Fifth Vial; poured upon the seat of the Beast.
The seat of the Beast; is the center of his power, authority, and influence. The followers of the Beast will suffer unbearable pains, that they gnawed their tongues for pain. But they still will not repent.

"And blasphemed the God of heaven because of their pains and their sores, and repented not of their deeds." (Revelation 16:11).

This vial has to do with the imposition of darkness on the center of the Beast's power, anticipating the destruction of the empire that claims to be the Kingdom of the Messiah.

The Sixth Vial; poured out upon the Great River Euphrates.
Three unclean spirits like frogs; loathsome, creeping, and unclean things.
The dragon; the devil.
The Beast; the first Beast that rose up out of the sea (Revelation 13:1).
The false prophet; the second Beast that rose out of the earth, (Revelation 13:11) was in league with the first Beast, (Revelation 13:12-15) and worked miracles before him. That this Beast is here to be understood is certain from Revelation 19:20. Here then is represented a league between the civil and ecclesiastical persecuting powers under the direction of Satan, and the three frogs seem to be a general warfare against Christ and His people. This brings on the final decisive conflict so often foretold in holy writings, and again set forth in Revelation 19:11-12.
The sixth vial prepares the way for an invasion of Kings from the east, that they with the Beast's armies, might come to judgment of Armageddon.
The Seventh Vial; poured out into the air; the place of storms and tempests, which immediately follow, (Revelation 16:18,21) and are as well as earthquakes, symbolic of mighty commotions and over-turnings among the nations.
It is done; the destruction of the enemies of God is complete.

> "And there fell upon men a great hail out of heaven, every stone about the weight of a talent; and men blasphemed God because of the plague of the hail; for the plague thereof was exceeding great." (Revelation 16:21)

A great hail; a symbol of God's awful judgment on the wicked.
The weight of a talent; the attic talent was equal to about fifty-seven pounds; the Hebrew talent to more than a hundred pounds. The weight of the stones represents the awful severity of the judgments. The seventh vial has to do with a great convulsion that completely overthrows the ordered affairs of men as they experience the fierceness of his wrath (Revelation 16:19).

After the accomplishment of the mystery of God by the pouring out of the seventh vial, the Prophet has a further and more particular vision of the same great persecuting power whose doom has been foretold. He carried by one of the seven angels into the wilderness, and then sees a harlot riding upon a scarlet-colored beast, which is manifestly the same as the Beast that rose out of the sea (Revelation 13:1). A harlot is the appropriate symbol of an apostate church, and her riding upon the beast represents the fact that the beast supports her, and she uses it for the accomplishment of her base purposes. She is therefore the same for substance as the two-horned best that "exerciseth all the power of the first beast before him." (Revelation 13:11,12) One of the seven angels which had the seven vials, showed the Prophet John the judgment of the great whore.

## The Twenty-One Divine Judgments of God

The First Seal
The Second Seal
The Third Seal
The Fourth Seal
The Fifth Seal
The Sixth Seal
The Seventh Seal

           The First Trumpet
           The Second Trumpet
           The Third Trumpet
           The Fourth Trumpet
           The Fifth Trumpet
           The Sixth Trumpet
           The Seventh Trumpet

                        The First Vial
                        The Second Vial
                        The Third Vial
                        The Fourth Vial
                        The Fifth Vial
                        The Six Vial
                        The Seventh Vial

# CHAPTER XIII
# THE JUDGMENT ASSOCIATED
# WITH THE SECOND ADVENT

The scriptures anticipate a coming judgment by God on all men:

> ". . . for He cometh, for He cometh to judge the earth; He shall judge the world with righteousness, and the people with truth. (Palms 96:13)

Also Apostolic Paul states:

> "Because He hath appointed a day in the, which He will judge the world in righteousness by that man whom He hath ordained; whereof He hath given assurance unto all men, in that He hath raised him from the dead. (Acts 17:31)

I.   The judgment of the cross

(1) <u>Hearth my word</u>; receiveth my instructions and treateth them as true.
    <u>Hath everlasting life</u>; the beginning of that spiritual life witch shall continue and increase forever.
    <u>From death unto life</u>; from a state of sin and guilt to a state of holiness and bliss (JN 5:24)

(2) <u>Being now justified by His blood</u>; the argument is from the less to the greater: if while we were yet enemies to God an expiation was made for our sins, much more now that through that expiation was made for our sins, much more, now that through that expiation we have

been brought into an actual state of justification, shall we be saved from that God's wrath. (Romans 5:9)

(3) No condemnation; from God.

Who walk; live habitually.

Not After the flesh; not as corrupt nature prompts, seeking supremely earthly good and selfish gratification.

After the spirit; as the Holy Spirit directs, regarding principally God, Christ, heaven and spiritual, eternal things. (Romans 8:1)

(4) (To be sin; suffer to make atonement for it. In giving His Son to die for His enemies, and in loving by the gospel through His ministers, and beseeching men to be reconciled to Him, God has shown that He is exceeding desirous of their salvation; and that if any are lost, it will be because they refuse to be reconciled to him. (II Corinthians 5:21).

(5) The curse of the Law; the punishment which it threatens against transgressors.

Made a curse; treated as accursed, in suffering for our sake the cursed death of the cross (Galatians 3:13; Deuteronomy 21:23).

(6) The end of the world; in the end of the ages; in those last days by which the Hebrew prophets represented the then distant future of a Christian dispensation.

To put away sin; to expiate it, and open the way for deliverance from its punishment, pollution, and power.

As it is appointed unto men; he points out in these words the agreement between the one death of men who are to be redeemed, and the one death of their redeemer, the man Christ Jesus.

To bear the sins of many; to die or account of them, in the room and stead of sinners; the just for the unjust.

Them that look for Him; His people, who expect His coming to judgment.

Without sin; not as before to suffer for sin, but to give His people free, full and everlasting salvation (Hebrews 9:26-28).

(7) By the which will; of God as done by Christ, especially in His suffering and death, believers are justified and sanctified. Jesus Christ crucified, as an atonement for sin, is the great subject of the Old Testament scriptures. Their principles and precepts, their rites and ceremonies, their sacrifices and offerings, their predictions, declarations and promises have reference to him; and one who does not see them in this light will never apprehend the fullness or duly appreciate the perfection of their meaning. (Hebrews 10:10; 14-17)

II. The Judgment on the Believer is Chastening

(1) <u>If we would judge ourselves</u>; properly examine and decide concerning ourselves.
<u>We should not be judged</u>; no punished of the Lord
<u>Not be condemned</u>; the object of God in chastising His children in this world is to lead them to repentance and reformation that they may not in the future world be condemned. (I Corinthians 11:31-32).

(2) <u>Chastening</u>; trials designed to correct your faults and make you better. God never sends trials because He has any pleasure in afflicting His people, but to make them more useful and happy than they would be without them. Therefore, a cheerful and hearty submission is required not only by the glory of God, but by our own high good. (Hebrews 12:7)

III. The Self Judgment of the Believer

(1) <u>Confess our sins</u>; to God, and forsake them (Proverbs 28:13)
<u>Faithful</u>; to be promises of forgiveness to the penitent. (Proverbs 28:13)
<u>Just</u>; to himself and all the great interests of His kingdom.
<u>Cleanse us</u>; from the guilt and the defilement of sin, so as at last to present us spotless before the throne of His glory with exceeding joy. (Jude 24; I John 1:9)

(2) <u>Ingenuous confession of sin and hearty turning from it are essential to forgiveness</u>; and those who will not confess and forsake it, must suffer its dreadful consequences forever (Psalms 32:5)

IV. The Judgment of the Believer's Works at the Judgment Seat of Christ

(1) <u>Of Christ</u>; our rightful and proper Judge. (Romans 14:10)

(2) <u>Made manifest</u>; shown to be what it really is.
<u>The day</u>; the day of judgment will make it known.
<u>Revealed by fire</u>; as fire shows the difference between gold and wood, or silver and stuble, so the day of judgment will show the difference between the works of different men. (I Corinthians 3:11-15)

(3) <u>Judge nothing before the time</u>; namely when the Lord shall come to judgment, as immediately afterwards stated. In the meantime, they were not to decide upon and condemn the character of one another.
<u>Hidden things of darkness</u>; those which are not seen of men.
<u>Counsels of the hearts</u>; desires, intentions and motives.

Have praise of God; for all that he has done well. The Apostle states only one side of the Judgment – the approval of those who have been faithful to Christ. The condemnation of the unfaithful is implied in this. (I Corinthians 4:5)

(4) An abiding conviction; that each individual will stand at the Judgment Seat of Christ, and receive according to the deeds done in the body, is adapted to make men circumspect, and lead them most earnestly to desire and diligently to labor that they may be accepted of Him. (II Corinthians 5:10)

# CHAPTER XIV
# THE JUDGEMENT OF THE NATIONS

At the time when God's re-gathering of Israel to the Land, He will gather all nations into the Valley of Jehoshaphat to judgment. The site indicated must be in or near Jerusalem. The method of god's gathering of the nations to the judgment is set forth in Jeremiah 3:9-12; one of the most important features of the judgment is the basis of it. The nations will be judged for God's people and for His heritage Israel. The great sin of the nations, all will be involved in, is in the time of Jacob's Trouble (Jeremiah 30:7). Little do the nations realize how they incur the wrath of God when they lay violent hands upon His heritage and the plant of His choosing. Joel shows the reckoning has come because Israel was scattered among the nations; their land was divided. God calls upon the nations to prepare for war; this is the method whereby He brings these nations to their deserved judgment. (I Samuel 7:8-9; Jeremiah 6:4). This is to be war to the finish. To that end, let all the nations muster and mobilize their manpower to the very hilt. Let them come fully equipped and accoutered. The nations will be banded together and confederate as never before (Psalms 2:1-3). The nations are seen as bestirring themselves to the white heat of wrath against Israel. Their objective is the Valley of Jehoshaphat (Jehovah judges). Just as the Lord speaks to the nations in Jeremiah 3:12, so, He commands His agents of judgment. The judgment is described under the double figure of the harvest and the vintage. The harvest is ripe, and the winepress and vats are full to overflowing. This judgment is referred to in Isaiah 63:1 and prominently in Revelation 14:14-20. Terrific will be the impact when God's mighty ones meet the mighty ones of the nations in mortal and final combat. The lifeblood of the nations will drench the soil of the earth. The prophet sees the nations assembled in innumerable hosts in the valley where God will make His decision. The repetition of the word multitudes is meant to show how innumerable they are. The valley of decision defines more clearly the Valley of Jehoshaphat. There the words of decision, "Come, ye blessed of my Father" and "Depart, ye cursed." (Genesis 12:1-3), will be uttered with the voice of the mighty Son of God, voice as the sound of many waters. Heaven and earth will feel the force of this judgment.

The judgment on nations, however, is never meant to be an end in itself. Through it, God means to bring blessings to His people Israel. The Prophets Isaiah, Jeremiah and Ezekiel also have prophecies against foreign nations, but they place such oracles after the indictments against God's own people Israel. Judgment will fall first upon Damascus, the capital of Syria, the nations chosen. Syria was to be visited for her cruelties to Israel. After Christ has dealt with the enemies, He will gather together the nations for judgment. It should be noted that the sheep go into the Kingdom, and the goats into eternal punishment (Matthew 25:31-46; Joel 3:11-17 and II Thessalonians 1:7-10). Matthew 25:31-46 states that this judgment will take place at the coming of Christ with His saints. Notice three things in this chapter:

(1) The marriage supper of the Lamb (verses 1-13)
(2) The judgment of the saints (verses 14-30)
(3) The judgment of the living nations (verses 31-46)

This is not a general judgment of good and bad. The church no more belongs to the nations than does Israel; for there are three classes here. The nations are those who deal with Israel through the great tribulation. The "brethren" are probably the Jewish remnant who have turned to Christ during the Great Tribulation and whom the antichrist has several persecuted as also have many of the wicked nations. This is a judgment of nations that are living; there is no mention of the dead.

The judgment of the living nations, I believe to be those nations remaining on the earth, who were not present as combatants at Armageddon. Armageddon is a place in the large, plain of Esdraelon, west of the river Jordan. In biblical times the place was called Megiddo; the famous battlefield in Northern Palestine where the Egyptians, Assyrians and Babylonian armies fought over the supremacy in Palestine and Syria. Josiah, King of Judea, was slain at Megiddo by Pharoah-nechoh, King of Egypt, when the former went to the help of Assyria, against Egypt (II Kings 23:29-30). Armageddon, or as it is called in Hebrew, Har-megiddo was the meeting place of the rival armies. Armageddon is chosen as the battlefield for the final struggle between the forces of good and the forces of evil.

In ancient times, the place was noted for battles; it was a familiar battleground and the gateway to Syria and the Euphrates Valley. The kings of the earth and of the whole world are to be gathered together through the activity of the trinity from hell to what is called "the battle of the great day of God Almighty (Revelation 16:14). This confluence of the nations of the earth is in a place called Armageddon.

"And he gathered them together into a place called in the Hebrew tongue Armageddon." (Revelation 16:16)

Armageddon is a place in the large, plain of Esdraelon, west of the River Jordan. In biblical times, the place was called Megiddo; the famous battlefield in Northern Palestine where the Egyptian, Assyrian and Babylonian armies fought over the supremacy in Palestine and Syria. Josiah, King of Judea, was slain at Megiddo by Pharoah-Nechoh, King of Egypt, when the former went to the help of Assyria, against Egypt (II Kings 23:29-30). Armageddon, or as it is called in Hebrew Har-megiddo, was the meeting place of the rival armies. Armageddon is chosen as the battlefield for the final struggle between the forces of good and the forces of evil. The battle is symbolic of the great contest between the forces of good and those of evil. The good will ultimately triumph and the blood of the saints will be avenged. There God deals in judgment with the nations because of their persecution of Israel (Joel 3:2); because of their sinfulness (Revelation 19:15), and because of their godlessness (Revelation 16:9). The Battle of Armageddon is an isolated event transpiring just prior to the second coming of Jesus Christ to the earth.

Isaiah states:

"I have trodden the winepress alone; and of the people there was none with me: For I will tread them in mine anger, and trample them in my fury; and their blood shall be sprinkled upon my garments, and I will stain all my raiment. For the day of vengeance is in mine heart, and the year of my redeemed is come. And I looked, and there was none to help; and I wondered that there was none to uphold: Therefore, mine own arm brought salvation unto me; and my fury, it upheld me. And I will tread down the people in mine anger, and make them drunk in my fury, and I will bring down their strength to earth. (Isaiah 63:3-6)

In the Battle of Armageddon, all nations are engaged (Joel 13:2; Zephaniah 3:8; Zechariah 12:3; 14:4). At Armageddon, the armies come from the whole earth to destroy the people of God, at Armageddon. There is no protest for all nations are joined against Jerusalem, at Armageddon the beast is the head of the invasion (Revelation 19:19). The armies at Armageddon are destroyed by the sword that goes out of Christ's mouth (Revelation 19:15). At Armageddon Jesus Christ is viewed as treading the winepress alone.

> "And the winepress was trodden without the city, and blood came out of the winepress, even unto the horse bridles, by the space of a thousand and six hundred furlongs." (Revelation 14:20)

An Eastern winepress is about ten feet in diameter and two and a half to three feet deep, constructed of bricks and inlaid with cement or clay. Grapes are put in it and trodden under the feet of men. The juice drains out through a narrow passage and is caught in earthen jars or skin containers. In the vision, the winepress was so large that the grapes were trodden under the feet of horses, just as oxen are used in treading wheat. The winepress was a thousand and six hundred furlongs. Wine is symbolic of drunkenness and destruction. The Apostle points out that in the latter days, the people would be drunk with pride and hatred, and that as a result, suffering and destruction would prevail everywhere. The upheaval would be wrought by men themselves. The world would be drunk with human pride, selfishness and other evils that are distasteful in the sight of God, and which results in destruction and human suffering will come to an end. The Gentile rule will be overthrown, and a new Jerusalem will rise in place of the old. The true religion will be restored and the Holy City will once more become the center of worship.

Political Israel came to an end with the Babylonian captivity, but the spiritual Israel was crushed under the Roman rule when the Temple was destroyed by Titus in A.D. 70. Jesus had predicted the destruction of the Holy City and the Temple:

> "And Jerusalem shall be trodden down of Gentiles, until the time of the Gentiles is fulfilled." (Luke 21:24)

The days of the Gentiles are numbered. They will come to an end. The remnant, or the spiritual Israel will be restored by the Messiah, who in due time will establish the Kingdom of God and His righteousness on earth. The Jews will return to their homeland. The scattered remnant of Israel will be gathered. The glory of God will once more shine from Jerusalem.

I suggest that the final judgment on the living nations take place at the middle of the Tribulation. The invasion takes place at a time when Israel is dwelling in their land (Ezekiel 38:8). Thus the Battle of Armageddon begins at the middle of the Tribulation to just prior of the Millennium.

# CHAPTER XV
# THE JUDGEMENT OF ISRAEL

In the parable of the Ten Virgins, the Lord is indicating that following the re-gathering of Israel, (Matthew 24:31) the next event will be the judging of living Israel on the earth to determine who will go into the Kingdom. This has been anticipated in Matthew 24:28, where unbelieving Israel is likened unto a lifeless corpse which is consigned to the vultures, a picture of judgment.

In the first half of the tribulation period, Israel will experience the chastisements of the events of the seals of Revelation, chapter 6. In the middle of the tribulation, persecution will break out (Revelation 12:12-17), because of the desolation (II Thessalonians 2; Revelation 13:1-10), who will cause Israel to flee from the land (Matthew 24:16-21). The Jews will make a covenant with the Antichrist for one week (seven years), which is seven of the Tribulation. In the middle of which they will break the covenant (Daniel 9:27; I Thessalonians 2). They will then pass through the Great Tribulation (Matthew 24:21,22,29; Revelation 3:10; 7:14); are converted (as a nation) at the second coming of Christ (Zechariah 12:10; Revelation 1:7); and become great missionaries (Zechariah 8:13-23).

Unbelieving Israel will be deceived by the false prophet (Matthew 24:11; Revelation 13:11-18), and go into apostasy (Matthew 24:12; II Thessalonians 2:11). Believing Israel will be a witnessing people carrying the good news that these events herald the approach of the Messiah (Matthew 24:14). Ezekiel saw in the historic events of Israel's past the very matrix and mold for events that still lie in the distant future. Having re-gathered His people from the corners of the earth, God will bring them into the wilderness of the people for the purpose of judging them. The judgment under consideration will be face-to-face without any intervening parties. He likened the coming judgment to God's dealings with their rebellious ancestors in the wilderness of the land of Egypt. As a Shepherd's staff is employed to count the sheep (Jeremiah 33:13), so the Lord will bring the entire flock under the Rod, this time with the purpose of separating the godly from the wicked (believing Israel from the unbelieving Israel). The godly will be brought more firmly into the bond of the covenant; whereas, the rebels will be purged out;; those who have transgressed against the Lord will be brought out of the land of their sojourn but denied admission to the Land of Promise (The Millennium). Just as Matthew, chapter 25 states, "in the judgment of the nations (an event which takes place in the same general prophetic period of the latter days for Israel), there is a separation of sheep individuals from goat individuals, so in this purging judgment on Israel. This is an exclusive judgment on Israel which will take place during the time of Jacob's trouble, probably at the end of the Tribulation period.

The point of Jesus in this parable is that God's final judgment will result in eternal separation between the righteous and the wicked. Final judgment will be based on what actual deeds are revealed about the true inner spiritual state of persons. Hypocrisy cannot survive the judgment. Final destiny for the unrighteous will be the company of the devil and his angels in everlasting fire, separated from God forever.

Jesus spoke of the parable of the Ten Virgins, which represent the remnant of Israel after the Church has been taken. The five wise virgins are the believing remnant, the five foolish virgins are the unbelieving remnant, who only profess to be looking for the Messiah's coming in power.

The major consideration in this parable seems to be in Matthew 25:10, "They that were ready went in with Him to the marriage-Feast-." Therefore, the Lord is teaching that, following the second coming and the re-gathering of Israel, there will be a judgment on the earth for living Israel to determine who will go into the Kingdom, and who will be excluded from it. Those with light will be admitted into The Millennium Kingdom, and those without light will be excluded from The Millennium Kingdom, which means that those with life are received and those without life are rejected.

In this present day of loose thinking, loose living and loose holding of religious convictions, it must be emphasized that the <u>God</u> of the Bible is a God of truth and judgment. He is no respecter of persons, as has been discovered by nation after nation that has contravened His law. The identical principle is operative for individuals as well.

Remember, Joel, the Prophet of old, whom Peter's words in Acts 2:17, "At that time God will pour out His spirit upon all flesh?" It will be universal in character and scope. We must not think that this is the first mentioned of an outpouring of the Spirit of God upon Israel in the Old Testament prophetic books, Isaiah 32:15; 44:3, 4; Ezekiel 36:37,28; 37:14; 39:29 and Zechariah 12:10. But that day will mean wrath and judgment upon the unbelieving. God will perform mighty transformations both in heaven and on earth. The sun and the moon will be affected; blood and fire (as in Exodus 7:17 and 9:24); and pillars of smoke (as in Exodus 19:19) will be visible. It will be the great and fearful Day of Jehovah. There will be those who call upon unto spiritual salvation. God has foretold that there would be an escaped remnant (Obadiah 17; Zechariah 14:1-5), and these will be a blessing to the whole earth. The prophesy of Joel was not fulfilled in Acts, chapter 2; "God should pour out His spirit upon all flesh." Peter saw in the events of his day proof that God would yet completely bring to pass all that Joel prophesized. Joel's prophecy, then, was prefilled; it is yet to be fulfilled; no Prophet in the Old Testament has a more important revelation of the end times than Joel, chapter 3. How gracious of God to let us know the exact time of these happenings. They will take place when the Lord Himself returns the captivity of Judah and Jerusalem. The return of Israel to the Land will never be fully accomplished until the Lord does it by His omnipotent power.

# CHAPTER XVI
## THE JUDGMENT OF THE GENTILES

The time of the judgment of the Gentiles is seen to follow the judgment upon Israel (Matthew 24, 25). This judgment takes place following the coming of Christ to the earth. Joel states:

> "For, behold, in those days, and in that time when I shall bring again the captivity of Judah and Jerusalem, I will also gather all nations and will bring them down into the Valley of Jehoshaphat, and will plead with them there for my people and for my heritage Israel, whom they have scattered among the nations, and parted my land (Joel 3:12)."

The prophet reveals that this judgment on the Gentiles will take place at the same time that the Lord restores the nation Israel to their land, which is at the second coming of Jesus Christ. Therefore, this judgment must fall at the time of the second coming after the re-gathering and judgment on Israel. It must precede the institution of the millennium, for those accepted in this judgment are taken into that Kingdom (Matthew 25:34). Jesus Christ was the humble suffering servant in His earthly ministry, He will return as the all powerful King executing final judgment. At the time of God's re-gathering of Israel to the land, He will gather all nations into the Valley of Jehoshaphat to judgment. The name Jehoshaphat means "Jehovah Judges." This judgment seems to be a judgment on the living Gentiles at the second coming of Jesus Christ. Some of the Gentiles will be saved during the Tribulation. These Gentiles are judged on the basis of their works to determine whether they are saved or lost as they have received or rejected the preaching of the gospel by the remnant during the Tribulation period. The living Gentiles will be judged as individuals; any message given is given expecting a personal response.

The basis on which judgment is meted out at this judgment is the treatment received by a group called "my brethren" (Matthew 25:40, 45). According to the Book of Revelation, God will seal a believing group called the brethren, the 144,000 at the beginning of the tribulation period. They will be a witnessing remnant for that entire period and the fruits of their ministry are described in Revelation 7:9-17:

> "After this I beheld, and, lo, a great multitude, which no man could number, of all nations, and kindred, and people, and tongues, stood before the Lamb, clothed with white robes, and palms in their hands; And cried with a loud voice, saying, salvation to our God which sitteth upon the throne, and unto the Lamb. And all the angels stood round about the throne, and about the elders and the four beasts, and fell before the throne on their faces, and worshipped God, saying, Amen: Blessings, and glory, and wisdom, and thanksgiving, and honor, and power, and might be unto our God forever and ever Amen. And one of the elders answered saying, "Unto me, what are these which are arrayed in while robes? And whence came they?" And I said, "Unto Him, Sir, Thou knowest." And he said to me, "These are they which came out of the Great Tribulation." And have washed their robes, and made them white in the blood of the Lamb." (Revelation 7:9-14)

The great multitude here represents the remnant of those who are to be saved of the Gentile nations. The people of all races from the four corners of the earth are to sit with Abraham, Isaac and Jacob in the Kingdom of God. "Clothed with white robes" suggests that this multitude has been purified. Both Jews and Gentiles who believe in Him are to participate in His second coming. There will be a remnant from all races and tongues which will greet Him at His coming.

> "Behold, the Lord cometh with ten thousand of His saints, to executive judgment upon all, and to convince all that are ungodly among them of all their ungodly deeds which they have ungodly committed, and of all their hard speeches which ungodly sinners have spoken against Him." (Jude 14-15)

This judgment is separating the unsaved from the saved prior to the millennium, it is an individual judgment as in the parallel references to the judgment at the end of the age in connection with the second coming seem to be individual judgments (Matthew 13:30; Matthew 13:47-50). There will be a twofold result of the judgment on the living Gentiles.

(1) To those who have been appointed to the King's right hand, the invitation is extended. "Come, ye blessed of my Father, inherit the kingdom prepared for you from the foundation of the world." (Matthew 25:34)

(2) To those consigned to the King's left the judgment is pronounced, depart from me, ye cursed into everlasting fire, prepared for the devil and his angels. (Matthew 25:41)

This group of Gentiles taken into the Kingdom fulfills the prophecies, (Daniel 7:14; Isaiah 55:5 and Micah 4:2) that states that a great group of Gentiles will be brought under the King's reign.

During the period of the ministry of the brethren, "this gospel of the Kingdom shall be preached in all the world for a witness unto all nations." (Matthew 24:14) This gospel of the Kingdom is the preaching of the death of Christ and the blood of Jesus Christ, as the way of salvation. The Gentiles at this judgment were received or rejected on the basis of their reception or rejection of the gospel that was preached by the brethren. Those who accepted their gospel accepted the messenger and those who rejected their gospel rejected the messenger. The Lord had said,

"Except ye be converted and come as little children, ye shall not enter into the Kingdom of heaven." (Matthew 18:3)

The Gentile nations heard the good news of the gospel of the Kingdom for the first time through the 144,000 redeemed children of Israel. When the disciples of Jesus Christ asked Jesus Christ what would be the sign of His coming and of the end of the age, He said,"

"And this gospel of the Kingdom shall be preached in all the world for a witness unto all nations (Gentiles); and then shall the end come." (Matthew 24:14)

I believe Jesus Christ meant the end of "The Tribulation" (Matthew 24:29; Daniel 7:21-25; 9:24-27). This "Great Multitude" of Revelation 7:9-17 are the sheep nations of whom Jesus Christ spoke in Matthew 25:31-40. The 144,000 (the brethren) witnessing Israelites will be persecuted for their testimony. They will be hungry, thirsty, in need of clothing and cast into prison. But those Gentiles who believe their message will stand with them and minister to them, so that it is to them Jesus Christ will say:

"In as much as ye have done it unto one of the least of these <u>my brethren,</u> ye have done it unto me." (Matthew 25:40)

This multitude will be preserved through the tribulation. These elect-Gentiles will be <u>saved</u> during the period of tribulation, because of the message of "The Brethern.", the 144,000 Jewish missionaries. There will be a two-fold result of the judgment on the living Gentile nations. Those who heard and excepted the message of the witnessing (the Brethern) and those who did not:

The Gentile rule comes to an end at the end of the Tribulation period and just before the Millennium.

"And the great city was divided into three parts, and the cities of the nations fell: and great Babylon came in remembrance before God, to give unto her the cup of the wine of the fierceness of His wrath." (Revelation 16:19)

"Babylon" is used allegorically, meaning "The Gentile World." Babylon was noted for its wealth, luxuries, corruption and worldliness. The great city is depicted as the center of corruption and mother of harlots (Revelation 17:5). This is because the period of the Gentile power began with the destruction of Jerusalem by the Chaldean army, and the Babylonian captivity. Jerusalem, the Holy City of God, became subject to pagan Babylonian Kings and later to the Persians, Greeks, Romans, Arabs and Turks. The temple was destroyed and the worship was interrupted for a long period. When the Lord comes in glory, this period will come to an end. The Gentile rule will be overthrown, and a new Jerusalem will rise in place of the old one. The true religion will be restored and the Holy City will once more become the center of worship.

Political Israel came to an end with the Babylonian captivity, but the spiritual Israel was crushed under the Roman rule, when the temple was destroyed by Titus in A.D. 70. Jesus had predicted the destruction of the Holy City and the temple:

"And Jerusalem shall be trodden down of the Gentiles until the time of the Gentiles is fulfilled." (Luke 21:24)

The days of the Gentiles are numbered. They will come to an end. The remnant, of the spiritual Israel, will be restored by the Messiah who in due time will establish the Kingdom of God and His righteousness on earth. The Jews will return to their homeland. The scattered remnant of Israel will be gathered. The glory of God will once more shine from Jerusalem.

The judgment is on the system called "The Great Whore" or harlot (Revelation 17:1). It is a combination of apostate Protestantism, Romanism and Atheism. It is the huge ecumenical church of the last days. It is doomed and must come under the judgment of God. A church which calls itself Christian, and which courts an alliance with the godless world-system, commits spiritual adultery (James 4:4). God calls her a harlot. In <u>Revelation 17:1</u>, her judgment is pronounced. The judgment upon the great whore, then, is a divine judgment upon apostate religion as a wife who is unfaithful to her husband. This great whore or harlot may claim to be the Bride of Christ, but she proves to be an adulteress who is unfaithful. Her illicit intercourse, with the world-system is contrary to the behavior of Christ's true church. His church is a called-out-assembly to be separated from the world (Acts 15:14; Romans 12:2; I John 2:15; James 4:4). The "Great Harlot", the apostate religious system of the last days, forms an unholy intrigue with the political leaders of the earth.

But John is permitted to see the bloody martyrdoms to take place at the hands of the harlot at the close of the tribulation. Babylon has not changed. She continues to the end as she began in Genesis. This we should expect for it she loves the world, she will hate the saints who "love not the world (system), (I John 2:15), and will rejoice in their death.

<u>In Revelation 18:1-3</u>, the announcement of Judgment is made on the downfall of Babylon. She has been full of everything that God hates, the time of her destruction has arrived. She "is become the habitation of devils" (Demons) (Revelation 18:2). Babylon is a religious system, which claims to be Christ's true church, houses demons, whose abode is the abyss in the underground world. The true church is the habitation of God through the Holy Spirit (Ephesians 2:22), but Babylon has become "the hold of every foul spirit; the spirit of the world (I Corinthians 2:12); the spirit that now worketh in the children of disobedience (Ephesians 2:2); the spirit of error (I John 4:6); the spirit of bondage (Romans 8:15); and the spirit of man (I Corinthians 2:11). There are many foul spirits contending for the mastery of man's mind. We need to take heed to the admonition, beloved, believe not every spirit, but try the spirits whether they are of God: because many false prophets are gone out into the world (I John 4:1).

She (Babylon-the anti-God system) will be judged because she worshipped wealth and luxury, playing harlot to the great merchants of the world. She will be judged because she led many astray with her witchcraft and doctrines of demons, her spirits and necromancy, her bewitching attractiveness by which she lured the world to her feet. She will be judged because of the untold number of victims whom she slaughtered in the inquisition and in St. Bartholomew's massacre. She must pay for those shocking murders and for the many bloody persecutions which followed.

# CHAPTER XVII
# THE JUDGMENT ON THE
# FALLING ANGELS

"For if the word spoken by angels was stedfast, and every transgression and disobedience received a just recompense of reward." (Hebrews 2:2)

The angels who disobeyed the word of God are called "Fallen Angels." They were deposed from their rank and place, bound with chains, kept in darkness, and reserved for final judgment. According to the Prophet Isaiah, this group of angels lost first place and fell from grace because of pride and self-exaltation. He apparently considered Lucifer, son of the morning star, as their chief representative (Isaiah 14:12-13). Jesus referred to this incident when He said, "I beheld satan as lightening fall from heaven." (Luke 10:18) In Genesis, satan is represented by the serpent who was more subtle than any beast of the field (Genesis 3:1). Fallen angels and the wicked are to face everlasting condemnation. "Depart from me, ye cursed, into everlasting fire, prepared for the devil and his angels (Matthew 25:41). At times, fallen angels are symbolical of sons of God who have fallen from grace. Paul warns the believer to keep steadfast and loyal in the true teachings, lest they fall from grace and lose the salvation which they had obtained through Jesus Christ. For if God had not spared the angels, how can He spare those who are disobedient? (II Peter 2:4)

The falling angels will be judged after the millennial period is over, but just prior to the judgment of the Great White Throne. Jude states:

"And the angels which kept not their first estate, but left their own habitation, he hath reserved in everlasting chains under darkness unto the judgment of the great day." (Jude 6)

They left their own habitation; became discontented with their condition and refused to do the will of God, in the place assigned to them, II Peter 2:4, which states:

"For if God spared not the angels that sinned, but cast them down to hell, and delivered them into chains of darkness, to be reserved unto judgment."

Judgment comes on the fallen angels for their one sin of following satan in his rebellion against God (Isaiah 14:12-17; Ezekiel 28:12-19). All those on whom this judgment is meant, are consigned to the Lake of Fire forever. These falling angels will be judged with the devil, the beast and the false prophets. Revelation 20:10 states,

"And the devil that deceived them was cast into the Lake of Fire and brimstones, where the beast and the false prophet are, and shall be tormented day and night forever and ever." (Revelation 20:10)

But this will not take place until after the Millennium. The new covenant (Jeremiah 31:31) guarantees to all who enter this Millennium and who need salvation: (1) a new heart (Jeremiah 31:33); (2) the forgiveness of sins (Jeremiah 31:34); and (3) the fullness of the Spirit (Joel 2:28-29).

The Bible makes it clear in the New Testament that the new covenant is based on the blood of the Lord Jesus Christ (Hebrews 8:6; 10:12-18; Matthew 26:28). It may be affirmed that salvation in the Millennium will be based on the value of the death of Jesus Christ and will be appropriated by faith (Hebrews 11:6). Satan will be bounded for a thousand years, that is the duration of the Millennium, which is a 1,000 years. The Bible states,

-"And he laid hold on the dragon, that old serpent, which is the devil, and satan, and bound him a thousand years, and cast him into the bottomless pit, and shut him up, and set a seal upon him, that he should deceive the nations no more, till the thousand years should be fulfilled: and after that, he must be loosed a little season.

And when the thousand years are expired, satan shall be loosed out of his prison, and shall go out to deceive the nations which are in the four quarters of the earth, Gog and Magog, to gather them together to battle: the number of whom is as the sand of the sear. And they went up on the breadth of the earth, and compassed the camp of the saints about, and the beloved City; and fire came down from God out of heaven, and devoured them (Revelation 20:2-3; 7-9).

In order that the righteousness and peace might rule on earth, this evil one (satan) must be removed. At the close of the Great Tribulation, and just before Christ appears on the earth to bring in His kingdom, God sends an angel from heaven to bind satan. He comes with a "great chain in his hand" with which he binds satan for one thousand years. The place where satan is incarcerated during the Millennium is called "The Bottomless Pit." It also denotes the abyss, the immeasurable depth of the under-world, the lower regions, the intermediate abode of evil demons which are doomed forever. The bottomless pit, or abyss, is not the Lake of Fire, which is the final hell. It is a sort of prison house in which evil spirits are confined, awaiting the final judgment.

The Jews, having suffered under many foreign rulers, expected a period of peace and prosperity. This was to be the Messianic Kingdom. The pagan rulers were to be overthrown and God's rule restored. The work of restoration was entrusted to the Messiah who was expected to reestablish the realm of David and gather the scattered people of Israel. Since the destruction of the Temple by Titus in A.D. 70, the Jews have dreamed of a third Jewish common wealth. Easterners, when persecuted and misruled, dream of God's rule and His righteousness. Indeed, this dream of restoration and rehabilitation sustained the faith of every Jew, and strengthened them when everything seemed dark and hopeless. They also believed that injustices will finally be righted and the wicked punished, and consequently those who are persecuted and crushed will rise again to power and see their enemies suffer. The Jews look forward to what they call, "The Day of the Lord," that is the day of reckoning when every person will be rewarded according to his deeds.

The prophets predicted the destruction of the wicked, both the wicked Jews and the Gentiles. "The Lord maketh the earth empty, and maketh it waste, and turneth it upside down and scattereth abroad the inhabitants thereof. The land shall be utterly emptied, and utterly spoiled: for the Lord hath spoken this." (Isaiah 24:1, 3) The destruction is to be followed by a period of restoration and God's rule. "And the Lord shall be King over all the earth: in that day shall there be one Lord, and his name one." (Zechariah 14:9) Other prophets also predicted such a period of tribulation to be followed by a bright and hopeful future, a period of peace and prosperity. "They shall not hurt nor destroy in all my holy mountain: For the earth shall be full of knowledge of the Lord, as the waters cover the sea (Isaiah 11:9). The righteous will see the caucuses of the wicked who have transgressed against the Lord." (Isaiah 66:24) John, who is the author of the Book of Revelation, believed in the eventual restoration of Israel and the punishment of their enemies. The Millennium period, even though it is not mentioned in the four Gospels, was predicted by the Hebrew prophets and expected by the people throughout the centuries.

God's command at the Battle of Armageddon resulted in the defeat of the forces of evil and the beginning of the reign of peace. The dragon, (satan) is the material world of deception, ruled by the forces, which from the very beginning, have disputed God's authority and suppressed the truth. The evil will be brought under subjugation and ultimate destruction; that is, spiritual understanding and the light of the truth will fill the earth and darkness will disappear. The great victory will herald the beginning of the thousand years of peace and tranquility, the Millennium. During these years, the forces of evil will be inoperative and those who have suffered for the sake of justice will enter upon a new life. During these thousand years, God's truth and His authority will be supreme, the Gospel will be preached in all parts of the world for a witness unto all nations. Every individual will have an'[opportunity to know God and His truth. But still, some people will reject the word of God and rebel against His authority. The good and evil will remain until the last coming of the Lord, where the good and the wicked will be separated like a shepherd who separates the sheep from the goats. (Matthew 25:31-34)

According to Matthew's gospel, only one resurrection will take place at the second coming of Christ. This resurrection will be preceded by wars, revolutions, famines, earthquakes, and other tribulations. Jesus' second coming will be like that of a thief at night; no one will know the day and the hour. Immediately after the great signs and tribulations, the sun shall be darkened and the moon shall not give her light, and the whole system of the heavenly bodies will be destroyed. Then, the Son of Man will appear in the clouds of heaven with power and great glory. (Matthew 24:29-31)

According to the Gospels, all men will rise, the good and the bad, but the righteous will receive the reward of everlasting life, while the wicked will rise to receive judgment and punishment. When that time comes, all who are in graves shall hear Jesus' voice and come forth; they that have done good, unto the resurrection of life; and they that have done evil unto the resurrection of damnation." (John 5:28-29) The thousand years between the first and second resurrections is a period of peace and tranquility, which will be enjoyed by the righteous who were persecuted and deprived of joys while they were on this earth, living among the wicked. Satan shall be bound means that the forces of evil will become inoperative at least for a period of a thousand years. The one thousand years (Millennium) of Christ will begin with all redeemed (saved) people. No unsaved person will enter the Millennium (Isaiah 60:21; Joel 2:28). But, during the Millennium, children will be born of saved people, and then after having been born and reared in a perfect moral and spiritual society, they will be easily deceived by the devil, choosing to follow him while they turn their backs on Christ. Everyone that is born into this world is born with a sinful nature, because of Adam. Although the saved will go into the Millennium saved, they will still remain with a sinful nature. Because of that, children will be born with sinful natures in the Millennium. Evil nature, whether confined in a prison or subject to righteous rule, does not change. The carnal mind is enmity against God: For it is not subject to the Law of God, neither indeed can be, so then, they that are in the flesh cannot please God. (Romans 8:7-8) I believe that because of the sinful nature, people will still die.

"And it is appointed unto men once to die, but after this the judgment." (Hebrews 9:27)

After one thousand years, satan will be loosed out of his prison.

"And when the thousand years are expired, satan shall be loosed out of his prison." (Revelation 20:7)

Even after one thousand years of a righteous and peaceful reign, satan by his deception is able to discredit God's dealings and thereby lead the nations astray in a revolt against God. Those born during the Millennium will not be willing subjects of Christ, but will render mere lip service. They will love Him with their lips. Their subjection to Him will be by restraint, or restrained by Law. For just as soon as satan is released, they yield a ready allegiance to his deception.

The last big battle will take place, "God and Magog." Satan will inspire men to war against God. The attack is against Jerusalem, called "the beloved city" (Revelation 20:9). God's enemies are bent on destroying the place of Christ's throne on earth. But the attack is quickly ended when God sends fire from heaven to devour them. "For God is a consuming fire." (Hebrews 12:29) By this same means Gog and Magog are destroyed in the first great conflict (Ezekiel 38:22).

The purpose for which satan is released is readily discerned from his activity at the time of his loosing. When satan is chained, means that evil has been conquered and truth established. The chain is symbolic of truth and power, which restrains deception and violence. When truth and understanding dominates, evil is destroyed; and when evil prevails, the chain is broken and the wicked flourish. The thousand years of peace and tranquility will be once more disturbed by the forces of evil. The righteous will be given a trial. Many men will be mislead, but at last, the devil (deceiver) and the false prophet will be utterly destroyed. These events will be followed by the final resurrection (Revelation 20:13-15).

> "The age-long, adversary of humanity, faces eschatological defeat; the principle of defeat was accomplished at the cross (Hebrews 2:14). The preliminary manifestation of the defeat is seen in the binding of satan for one thousand years (Revelation 20:2-3). The final establishment of the eternal order is preceded by the endless confinement and torment of satan in the Lake of Fire (Revelation 20:7-10).

After the devil is thrown into the Lake of Fire, where the beast and the false prophet are, they will be tormented day and night forever and ever.

> "And the devil, who deceived them, was thrown into the lake of burning sulfur, where the beast and the false prophet had been thrown. They will be tormented day and night for ever and ever." (Revelation 20:10)

Then the final resurrection, for all unsaved, the Old Testament dead, the church age dead, the tribulation and millennium dead. This is the judgment on sinners. They will be resurrected to stand before God at the Great White Throne judgment.

# CHAPTER XVIII
# THE GREAT WHITE
# THRONE JUDGMENT

Right after God sends fire from heaven to devour them (Gog and Magog), by this means Gog and Magog are destroyed in the first great conflict (Ezekiel) the attack is quickly ended.

"For our God is a consuming fire." (Hebrews 12:29)

Before the Great White Throne appears all "the dead" (The judgment on sinners):

"And I saw the dead, small and great, stand before God; and the books were opened; and another book was opened, which is the Book of Life; and the dead were judged out of those things which were written in the books, according to their works." (Revelation 20:12)

Cases are tried under the laws which are contained in books. When a man is on trial, the Judge opens the book in the presence of the parties concerned, determines the guilt and prescribes the punishment. Every punishment and liability is prescribed. The first book is the Book of the Law which prescribes the punishment for crimes and the rewards for gallantry and good deeds. There is another book, the Book of Deeds and Records, where every man's acts are written down, justified in the case of Mordecai (Esther 6-11) These books are kept very carefully and are brought out only on special occasion, when difficult cases are tried. God gives everyone a charge to be ready:

"Behold, I come quickly: blessed is he that keepeth the sayings of the prophecy of this book." (Revelation 22:7)

Behold, I come quickly means, "I will come when I am not expected." Jesus told his disciples of His second and sudden coming. He assured them that he would be with them to the end of the world. Jesus did not set the hour and the time of His return. But His coming will be like a flash of light. Time has no meaning in divine terms. A thousand years are like a day with God. Those resurrected unto life have all been called out of the grave a thousand years earlier (Revelation 20:3-6). Those resurrected here are to be judged to be appointed unto the second death (Revelation 20:14); that is, eternal separation from the Kingdom of God. This is the final act in the program that was enacted that God may be all in all (I Corinthians 15:28):

"He that is unjust, let him be unjust still; and he which is filthy, let him be filthy still; and he that is righteous, let him be righteous still; and he that is holy, let him be holy still." (Revelation 22:11)

When the end will come, everyone will be caught up as he is. The unjust will be unjust, the filthy will be filthy, and the holy will be holy. That is to say, the end will come like a twinkle of the eye. What the writer means is that everyone will be caught unawares, as he is. The people will have no time to repent of their evil works. The coming of Christ will be so sudden that no one will have a chance to repent. He will come as a thief at night when no one expects him. (Revelation 16:15) This is why the Apostles admonish their followers to keep alert and be ready. They were judged, each one according to their works. And, if any was not found written in the Book of Life, he was cast into the Lake of Fire. Every dead (sinner) had to show up to be judged. Neither the sea nor the unseen world could any longer hide their prisoners. "And these gave up the dead that (were) in it, and death and Hades gave up the dead that were in them; and they were judged each one according to their works. Again, death and Hades are said to come to their end, personified as enemies. "And death and Hades were cast into the Lake of Fire. This is the second death, the Lake of Fire." This was concluded all dealing on the Lord's part with soul and body, and all that pertains to either. The race was now in the resurrection state either for good or for ill; and it must be forever. Death and Hades, which had so long been executions in a world where sin reigned; and still did their occasional office when righteousness reigned, themselves disappear where all traces of sin are consigned forever. God is still "all in all." God's purpose in the judgments prior to the Millennium was to "gather out of His Kingdom all things that offend, and them which do iniquity; and shall cast them into a furnace of fire: there shall be wailing and gnashing of teeth." (Matthew 13:41-42) God's purpose in the judgments at the end of the Millennium is to remove from the eternal Kingdom "all things that offend, and them which do iniquity." By this judgment, God's absolute sovereignty has now been manifested. The last judgment (The Great White Throne Judgment), will reveal our true righteousness. All our deeds will .lay open before God as He judges us. God has revealed that physical death is not the end of life. All the dead shall be called before God to give an account of their lives on earth. Death itself will be destroyed, but those not belonging to God's people will suffer the horrors of death forever, the Second Death. God will reveal Himself to all people in the judgment. The dead will appear before God on His throne to give an account of their actions, deeds, your thoughts, recorded out their lives, will be revealed. All will be judged according to the records of their daily living. The Second Death is identified with the Lake of Fire. It is a synonym for hell. It is second death in that it involves a final separation from God. All people die once. The wicked die a second time with no hope. The destiny of the lost is a place in the Lake of Fire (Revelation 19:20; 20:10; 14-15; 21:8). This Lake of Fire is described as everlasting fire (Matthew 25:41; 18:8), and as unquenchable fire (Mark 9:43-44, 46, 48), emphasizing the eternal character of the retribution of the lost.

> "But the fearful, and unbelieving and the abominable, and murderers and whoremongers, and sorcerers and idolaters, and all liars, shall have their part in the Lake which burneth with fire and brimstone; which is the Second Death." (Revelation 21:8)

Murder leads to eternal judgment, punishment, and separation from God. So do lying, and immorality. At the Judgment, God looks for obedient ones. The horrors of hell consist in the types of sinners to be found there, the torment of fire and brimstone, and the final or second death from which there is no escape to life.

<u>Abominable</u> – to pollute, to defile, to make detestable, to commit abomination; the word indicates persons whose very natures have been saturated with the abominations which they practice in their lifetime; and in this case, the abominations are not merely idolatrous acts, but the monstrous and unnatural vices of heathendom.
<u>Whoremongers</u> - immoral persons; one who practices sexual immorality.
<u>Sorcerers</u> – one who mixes and uses drugs, which are used either in sorcery or magic practices.

These were the wicked who did not have a part in the first resurrection. Now they will stand before the Great White Throne Judgment of God.

The Great White Throne Judgment is the final judgment of the unbeliever and takes place after the thousand year, Millennial, reign of Christ and the judgment of satan. The absolute purity of this supreme, court is symbolized by the color of the throne. The earth and heaven flee away before the awesome grandeur of God seated upon the Throne of Judgment. The books will be opened to judge those that are standing before the Judgment of God at the Great White Throne. The books indicate that which stands written. The sentence of the Judge is not arbitrary; it rests upon written evidence. The books which were opened contain, as it seems, a record of the deeds of every human being who came up for judgment.

As heaven is a place and not a mere state of mind, in like manner, those reprobated go to a place. This truth is indicated by the words <u>hades</u> (Matthew 11:23; 16:18; Luke 10:15; 16:23; Revelation 1:18; 20:13-14); and <u>gehenna</u> (Matthew 5:22, 29-30; 10:28; James 3:6), a place of torment (Luke 16:28). That is a condition of unspeakable misery indicated by the figurative terms used to describe its suffering, everlasting fire (Matthew 25:41); where their worn dieth not, and the fire is not quenched (Mark 9:44); bottomless pit (Revelation 9:2); outer darkness, a place of weeping and gnashing of teeth (Matthew 8:12); fire unquenchable (Luke 3:17); furnace of fire (Matthew 13:42); blackness of darkness (Jude 1:13), and the smoke of their torment ascendeth up for ever and ever; and they have no rest day nor night (Revelation 4:11).

In Matthew 25:41; the Lord said to the wicked, "Depart from me, be cursed, into everlasting fire, prepared for the devil and his angels." The word prepared literally is having been prepared, suggesting that the Lake of Fire is already in existence and awaiting its occupants. The word lake must connote a body of matter having liquid form. Therefore, if scripture is truth, this eternal fire must be in liquid form. We find, first, an eternal fire which cannot burn out. Being of a liquid consistency, it is secondly, a lake of fire. In the third place, it cannot be quenched, for any quenching material such as water, would immediately have its atoms stripped of electrons and be packed in with the rest. In the fourth place, since astronomers have been, and still are, studying this strange phenomenon, it is only too evident that the Lake of Fire has been prepared and is now ready. The resurrection body of the unsaved, evidently, will be of such character that it is indestructible even in the midst of such a lake of fire. Then, the final judgment, which is the Great White Throne Judgment, will produce the final destiny of the wicked.

Every view of the world has its eschatology. It cannot help raising the question of the which, as well as of the what and the whence. "O, my Lord!", said Daniel to the angel, "What shall be the end of these things?" (Daniel 12:8) What is the end, the final destiny of the individual? Does he perish at death, or does he enter into another state of being and under what conditions of happiness or woe does he exist there? What is the end, the final aim of the great whole, that far off divine event towards which the whole creation moves? The answer is that man shall be rewarded or punished. The wicked are to be punished:

(1) Eternal

The scriptures present the punishment of the wicked not only as "eternal" (or age-long), but as enduring "for ever and ever", or "unto the ages of ages." (Revelation 19:3; 20:10; 14:11)

(2) Punishment

"Then shall he say also unto them on the left hand depart from me, ye cursed, into everlasting fire, prepared for the devil and his angels." (Matthew 25:41) A place of anguish, tormenting, confinement in a strait place without relief.

(3) Fire

This is one of the most constant images under which the torment and misery of the wicked is represented. Fire is a symbol of the divine judgment of wrath (Matthew 5:22).

(4) Darkness

This word is used to describe the condition of the lost: cast into outer darkness; there shall be weeping and gnashing of teeth.

The wicked are thrust out from the light, joy, and festivity into the darkness and gloom without, as into the remote gloom and anguish of a dungeon in which are found agony, wrath, and despair separated from God (absence of spiritual light); separation from the company of the saved.

# BIBLIOGRAPHY

Holman. <u>Disciples' Study Bible</u>. New International Version: Nashville, Tennessee; Holman Bible Publisher

King James Version. <u>The Holy Bible</u>. Holman Bible Publishers: Nashville TN
Jay P. Green, Sr. <u>The Classic Bible Dictionary</u>. Sovereign Grace Trust Fund Lafayette: Indiana; 47903; 1988

J. Dwight Pentecost. <u>Things to Come</u>. Grand Rapids: Michigan; Zondervan Publishing House

William Evans. <u>The Great Doctrines of the Bible</u>. Chicago: Moody Press
<u>A Linquistic Key to the Greek New Testament</u>. Zondervan Publishing House: Grand Rapids; Michigan